ALONE
WITH GOD

ALONE WITH GOD

A MANUAL OF DEVOTIONS

J. H. GARRISON

Introduced and Edited by Gary Holloway

LEAFWOOD
PUBLISHERS

ALONE WITH GOD
A Manual of Devotions
published by Leafwood Publishers

Copyright © 2003 by Gary Holloway

ISBN 0-9728425-6-X
Printed in the United States of America

Cover design by June Steckler

For information:
Leafwood Publishers, Siloam Springs, AR
1-877-634-6004 (toll free)

Visit our website: www.leafwoodpublishers.com

03 04 05 06 07 08   7 6 5 4 3 2 1

CONTENTS

PART II. FORMS OF PRAYER

INTRODUCTION

All Christians pray. If, like me, you were "raised in the church," then prayer has always been part of your life. Some of my earliest memories are the prayers my parents taught me. I am thankful for that instruction in prayer, but for many years my prayer life did not go far beyond those childhood prayers. Although my prayers included praise and thanksgiving, they still primarily consisted of a list of concerns I wanted God to address.

Of course, it is always right to take our concerns to God, but lately I've come to want more from prayer. I want a deeper experience of the presence of God. I am not alone. A spiritual renewal is underway among those of the Stone-Campbell tradition. Partly that renewal is the result of living in an age that hungers for the spiritual. Perhaps another reason many Christians have discovered a thirst for a deeper experience of the presence of God is our history of debate and dispute. Tired of ill feelings and division over minor matters, we have determined (in the words of an earlier time) to dispute less and pray more.

In their search for a deeper spirituality, many have discovered spiritual classics from the Middle Ages to contemporary times. Are there such resources on spirituality from the Stone-Campbell heritage? Sadly, the answer is "Yes, but few." There are devotional writings from many of the leaders of the Stone-Campbell movement, but few are book-length. Leonard Allen has done a service to the church by making Robert Richardson's, *Communings in the Sanctuary* available again. This little volume of meditations and prayers adds to that heritage. Written over a hundred years ago by a recognized leader of the movement, these words of faith and praise resonate with the spiritual longings of our own age.

A "Sweet-spirited Religious Journal"

James H. Garrison (1842-1931), was one of the most influential leaders of the Stone-Campbell Movement in the period after the death of Alexander Campbell. For 62 years he was editor or regular writer of *The Christian-Evangelist*, a religious journal that became the official weekly paper of the Disciples of Christ. Through his weekly articles and his books, he shaped the church of his day.

Garrison was raised as a Baptist in southwestern Missouri, and was wounded fighting for the Union in the Civil War. After the war he attended Abingdon College in Illinois, a Disciples school run by graduates of Alexander Campbell's Bethany College. There he decided to join the Disciples. After graduating in 1868, he began to preach in Macomb, Illinois, and became co-editor of a religious paper, *The Gospel Echo*. In 1872, he moved to Quincy, Illinois, and merged his paper with *The Christian*. Settling in St. Louis in 1874, he merged his paper again in 1882, forming *The Christian-Evangelist*.

Although some in his day condemned him as a liberal,

others felt him too conservative. He refused to take an overly literal view of the Bible, but also stood against "Open Membership," that is, admitting the unimmersed to membership in the church. By contemporary standards, his theology is quite conservative.

Although he spoke on the disputed issues of his day, he tried to avoid unkind criticism of fellow Christians. Rejecting the "morbid fondness of controversy" that he felt had plagued Disciples, Garrison determined that his would be a "sweet-spirited religious journal." Perhaps more than anyone else in his generation, he was responsible for preserving both the high view of Scripture and the heritage of Christian unity of the early Stone-Campbell movement.

"That Realization of the Divine Presence"

Garrison also had strong feelings for the spiritual life, evidenced by a book-length study on the Holy Spirit, and by this volume, *Alone With God*, which proved to be his most popular work. *Alone With God* reflects Garrison's immersion in the devotional literature available to him. He quotes or adapts the writings of Thomas a Kempis (1380-1471), the *Book of Common Prayer*, and his contemporaries Lyman Abbott (1835-1922), Austin Phelps (1820-1890), William Landels (1823-1899), and Elizabeth Sewell (1815-1906). Scripture and hymns are his favorite sources. Interestingly, although he recognizes the contributions of a few contemporary "brethren," he does not quote from earlier Stone-Campbell writers.

Garrison's spirituality does seem out of step with many of his contemporaries from the Disciples of Christ and Churches of Christ. His was a controversial time, when these two groups became separate. It was a time of debate and division, a time heavily dependent on a narrow form of reasoning.

By contrast, Garrison's little book of meditations and prayers is filled with highly emotive language. He speaks of "deep and silent awe," "reverent intimacy," and "quiet meditation and communion with the invisible God." His approach fits well with the contemplative methods of St. John of the Cross (1542-1591) and the recent "Centering Prayer" method of Thomas Keating and others.

Of course the whole idea of written meditations and prayers was somewhat strange to his contemporaries among the Disciples and even more so to ours in Churches of Christ. In his preface, Garrison defends the value of written prayers. In his day and ours, many confuse thoughtless spontaneity with spirituality. There is certainly a role for extemporary prayer. But many today are discovering the depth and the discipline inherent in read prayer.

"Helpful to Those Who are Young in Christian Experience"

So how can this book lead you to a deeper experience of God? Garrison originally targeted this volume toward young Christians. If you are new to the faith, then you may find these meditations particularly helpful. However, some of us who have been Christians for years are still new to the experience of meditation, contemplation, and listening to God.

This book then can serve as a guide for personal daily devotion. The meditations are a powerful way to begin or end the day. Those beginning or continuing a period of daily family worship will also find them helpful. Small groups can use these meditations and prayers as ways of beginning or ending a study.

The second section of the book on forms of prayer will also aid in personal, family, and group meditation. They can also

help those who are called upon to lead prayer in congregation-
al assembly. We give too little thought and preparation to
those corporate, body of Christ, prayers.

In making these meditations and prayers available to a
new audience, I have modernized some spelling and vocabu-
lary, and have slightly modified the grammar (although I did
not thoroughly do so; one can still tell it is a nineteenth-centu-
ry document). Most changes were in the prayers in part two
of the volume, where I changed the archaic pronouns ("Thee,"
"Thine," "Thou," etc.) and verb forms ("art," "wouldst," etc.)
to make the prayers more readable. However I kept the Bible
quotations as they were, including "Thee's" and "Thou's." I
appreciate the help of Janis Adcock in making these changes.

So this is an invitation to hear the voice of God, to sit qui-
etly in his presence, to allow him to examine our hearts, to
experience his love and holiness. There are indeed no greater
moments of the day than those spent alone with God.

Gary Holloway
Nashville, Tennessee

PREFACE

This little volume owes its existence to numerous requests, especially from those young in years, or in Christian experience, for some work that would assist them in learning how to pray. Remembering that when the disciples came to Jesus with a similar request he did not refuse them, the author felt that it would be in harmony with the spirit of the Master's example to respond to this request in the best manner he could. I am not unaware of the prejudice that exists among us, in common with most Protestant bodies, against printed forms of prayer. Within certain limits, this aversion to forms is no doubt founded in reason. What is purely formal and perfunctory can have no value as worship. To read a prayer, or to say a prayer, is not necessarily to pray. To use forms without the spirit is the constant tendency in all worship, no less in song than in prayer.

And yet, forms are necessary. We could improvise our words in song, but printed hymns, carefully prepared, are much better, despite our tendency to forget the sentiments of the familiar lines. And while forms of prayer are not so essential as hymns for music, yet it cannot be doubted, I think, that they may be very helpful to young Christians, not only in teaching them the language of prayer, but especially in fostering the spirit of prayer. They may, also, give wider scope to our spiritual desires, and hence to our petitions. There is a proper use, as well as an abuse, of forms. In a letter from the late President W. H. Woolery, of Bethany College, touching this enterprise, he said: "I am really glad you are preparing a book of devotions. Our people need such a work. Carry it on to completion. You need not fear the criticism that ritualism will come from its use. Besides, our people could stand a little more ritual than they have. It is a nice point to know just how much form to use in worship. There are extremes both way, and we, if anything, are likely to err at the extreme of too little ceremony." There are very few among us who, having given this question much thought, would not endorse his words.

I will add, however, that it has not been my aim, in the preparation of this volume, to furnish forms of prayer for public worship, to be read out of the book, after the manner of the Episcopal Church. The forms given are intended to be suggestive and helpful to those who are young in Christian experience, and who have not yet learned to voice the newborn desires and emotions of the heart. It is believed that their study, in private, will be found very useful in cultivating a devotional spirit, as well as in acquainting young disciples with appropriate language in which to express their petitions. These forms will accomplish their purpose best in those who so use them as to become, after awhile, independent of them.

The author confesses to a feeling he has had for several years, that there is a great lack, among the rank and file of our membership, and not infrequently manifesting itself, also, in the ministry, of a devotional spirit. If it were germane to my present purpose, it would not be difficult to assign some reasons why this is so, but at present, I am concerned only with the fact itself. This lack is seen in the small number who attend our prayer meetings, the still smaller number who can be relied on to lead in prayer, the large number of homes in which there is no regular family worship, and in the unspiritual character of many of our church members. I institute no comparison between ourselves and others. There is reason to fear that the lack of which I am speaking, is far too general. This restless, rushing age, with its eager pursuit of wealth, honor and worldly pleasure, cannot fail to make its baneful influence felt on the spiritual life of the church. To contribute, in a very humble way, towards the neutralization of these adverse influences, and to point out, and stimulate my readers to attain, a higher standard of personal piety, has been my chief aim in the preparation of this work.

The book has a plan of its own which is different from that of any similar work, so far as I know. Part One contains a series of meditations on scripture passages designed to cover, in the main, our relations to God, and the privileges and duties growing out of these relations. Following each of these meditations, or studies, is a brief prayer, conceived in the spirit of the scripture that has been the theme of meditation. It has been my aim in this part of the work, to avoid, on the one hand, a severe, didactic style, as unsuited to the hour of devotion, and on the other, what might be called the "goody goody" style, which consists chiefly in pious platitudes, containing no solid instruction. In a word, I have tried to make these meditations both instructive and devotional. How far I have succeeded in this is for others to judge. Here, especially, I have kept constantly in mind the needs of the young, to help whom to the attainment of a high ideal of manhood and womanhood is a growing passion of my life. No higher compensation could I receive for whatever labor and time I have devoted to this work than the knowledge that it had been promotive of higher aims and ideals in my young readers.

The forms of prayer which follow under the title of "Private Devotions," are intended to cover a wide scope of our spiritual needs, and are adapted for personal use in the closet, where the "Father who sees in secret" will hear and reward openly. The original design of the work was limited to private devotions, consisting of the meditations and personal prayers, hence the title of the work. At the request of many, I have added the Family Worship and Special Occasion departments. While these do not fall strictly under the title, "Alone with God," I have thought best to let the name stand, and have added the subhead, "Manual of Devotions," which is broad enough to cover every feature of the book.

In the forms of prayer for "Private Devotions" and "Family Worship," I have made free use of the literature of prayer, so far as it was accessible to me, culling from every available source, and especially from the more ancient forms which have borne the test of long usage, but taking the privilege of cutting out, or altering, objectionable phrases, archaic forms of speech, and adding what seemed to be required to adapt them to their present use. By so doing, it is believed that a much more valuable collection of prayers has been secured than would have been possible in any other way. In the original forms here submitted there has been not the slightest attempt at rhetorical finish or flourish. Rather, the effort has been at plainness and simplicity of speech, which is more befitting the soul's intercourse with God.

It will perhaps be sufficient explanation of any imperfections which the reader may discover, either in the plan of the work, or in the manner in which it is carried out, if he will kind-ly remember that the author has had to prepare this volume in the fragments of time which he could gather up in the midst of his constantly pressing labors as editor of the *Christian Evangelist*, and with the additional limitation, during a great part of the time, of impaired health. But such as it is, and with all its imperfections, this little volume is now submitted to the charitable consideration of those for whom it is intended, with grateful remembrance of the favorable reception which was given to a former and not dissimilar work. Its preparation, even in the midst of other labors, has been a work of love, which has brought a rich blessing to my own heart. I can only pray that, under God, it may prove a blessing to all who examine its pages in a devotional spirit, and be found helpful in cultivating that "holiness, without which no man shall see the Lord."

J. H. Garrison
St. Louis, May 1, 1891

PART I

MEDITATIONS

"By all means; use sometimes to be alone. Salute yourself; see what your soul doth wear. Dare to look in your chest; for 'tis thine own; And tumble up and down what you findest there."

George Herbert

"We may lay it down as an elemental principle of religion, that no large growth in holiness was ever gained by one who did not take time to be often and long alone with God. This kind goeth not out without prayer and fasting. No otherwise can the great central idea of God enter into a man's life, and dwell there, supreme." Austin Phelps

"In the secret of His presence,
  How my soul delights to hide!
Oh, how precious are the lessons
  Which I learn at Jesus' side!
Earthly cares can never vex me,
  Neither trials lay me low,
For when Satan comes to tempt me,
  To the secret place I go."

E. L Gorch

1. The Silent Hour

And when he had sent the multitudes away he went up into a mountain apart to pray: and when the evening was come he was there alone.

MATT. 14:23

The busy day is ended. The shades of evening invite to repose. The gathering darkness woos the soul to meditation. How solemn is the night! The stars that look down upon us from their serene heights rebuke our fretfulness, and our undue absorption in the trivial concerns of this transitory life. They speak to us of that fair world where sin never blights, where death never invades, and where no shadow of sorrow ever falls. Let me, like the Master, retire awhile to solitude and give myself to meditation and prayer. O the quiet, holy joy of the silent hour, when the soul is alone with God! Have you learned to love it, dear reader? If not, you have yet to attain to one of the purest and sweetest pleasures possible to a Christian in this life. And our souls need the silent hour. Our contact with the visible world and with material things, necessary as it is, tends to deaden the finer sensibilities of our nature, and to impoverish the spirit, unless the influence is counterbalanced by seasons of quiet meditation and communion with the invisible God. God speaks to the soul in its moments of reverential silence. "Seldom find we a soul still enough to hear God speak." "My speech shall distill as the dew." Every day should have its quiet moments when, alone with God, the soul may meditate, with deep and silent awe, on everlasting things, and unbosom itself before the Father of spirits. This habit of reverent intimacy with God imparts that spiritual tone, that sensitiveness of conscience, that realization of the divine presence, so essential to moral beauty and symmetry of character. Shut in from the noise and scenes of the busy world, in the solitude of our chamber, we can the better examine our own hearts and give ourselves up to holier thoughts. "He, therefore, that intends to attain to the more inward and spiritual things of religion," says Thomas a Kempis, "must, with Jesus, depart from the multitude and press of people." Nor will there be any lack of time for this silent hour, if the fragments of hours, too often wasted on frivolous things, be gathered up for that purpose. No time to get ready for eternity? What, then, is time for? Lord, "so teach us to number our days that we may get us a heart of wisdom! "

Oh, how thoughtlessly the great mass of human beings are rushing on to eternity! Pressed by the demands of business, of pleasure and of society, how seldom do they take a quiet hour for reflection on their spiritual state and destiny! Perhaps it is not until the heavy hand of affliction is laid upon them that they pause in the mad pursuit of the world's prizes and pleasures, to hold converse with their own hearts. And even then, they find little enjoyment in these moments of introspection, so unaccustomed are they to being alone with God and their own conscience. It is like sitting in a strange room with strange company. The godless and the unthinking dislike to be alone. They have no company in their own thoughts, and know not how to commune with their own hearts. The giddy crowd, the unseemly jest, the hollow laughter of gay companions—these have far more attraction for them than thoughts about God, eternity, their own souls, their duty or their destiny. They relish more the society of the devotees of Pleasure, than of those whose "delight is in the law of the Lord." This is poverty in comparison with which the lack of mere worldly possessions is scarcely to be named.

Nor can it be denied that many professed Christians are living poor, lean, unspiritual lives, without any real relish for God's word, or for prayer, because of their habitual neglect of private meditation, self-examination and secret communings with God. And for this neglect, few of them can give any better excuse than the lack of time. There is time to look after the condition of the farm, the stock, the shop, the office and the markets, but no time to inquire into the condition of the soul and its fitness for eternity! Time to minister to the wants of the perishable body, but no time to look after the needs of the undying spirit! Can there be any greater delusion or self-deception than this? Is it not clearly one of the devices of Satan?

It is time that all such Christians should awaken from their slumber, and betake themselves to self-examination and prayer. O that every reader of these lines would resolve that, henceforth, in the calendar of daily duties, the lone hour with God shall have its place! Such a custom, once universally established, would work a glorious revolution in individual character, in family life, and in every department of Christian activity. It would fill the empty pews, increase the Sunday school, crowd the weekly prayer-meeting, supply the church treasury, swell the missionary offerings, furnish helping hands for weary and discouraged pastors, and raise the whole tone of church life and worship to a higher spiritual plane.

But this reform, like every other, must begin with individuals, and work, like leaven in the meal, until the whole mass be leavened. Will you begin at once this habit of private prayer, and meditation on some portion of God's word, and when you realize its personal benefits, commend it to others? To all who feel the impulse so to do, may God give strength to carry it into immediate practice!

Prayer

O you who hear prayer, bend low your ear to hear the faintest whisper of one of the weakest of your children. I come to you loving Father, because you have bidden me come, and because I feel my need of you. You, O God, alone can supply my needs. I am unworthy of the least of your mercies, but I come in the name of Jesus, and beseech you, for his dear sake, to hear and answer my prayer, and to accept my thanksgiving and praise, which I offer in his name. I thank you, most gracious Father, that you have called me into fellowship with you and with your Son, Jesus Christ, our Savior. I thank you for a place in your family, and the privilege of calling you Father, and feeling that you care for me, even me. And now, I beseech you, to grant that I may hunger and thirst after righteousness; that I may seek daily to feed on the divine manna which came down from heaven. O that my soul may be watered with the dews of your salvation! As you nourish all the living things of nature and cause them to grow, so, O Lord, wilt you nourish this soul of mine which you have created, and stir up within me new thoughts of duty and new desires of holiness. Cause me to delight in your word, in your house, in the communion of saints, in the fellowship of Christian work, and in prayer. May I learn to love and to look forward to these precious moments of communion with you, and to find here grace and strength for my daily need. In the plenitude of your mercy, O Father, forgive my past sins and strength-

en me with might by your Spirit in the inner man, that I may overcome all my evil inclinations and triumph over every evil habit. So
feeding on your word, meditating on your goodness, and communing with you, may I grow up into the image of him who is our
living head, even Jesus Christ. And this I ask for his name's sake.
Amen!

2. The Soul's Desire For God

As the hart panteth after the water-brooks, so panteth my soul after thee, O God!   Ps. 42:1

In these words, David has expressed the desire of every pious soul. Who, that has ever drunk of the water of life, can ever be satisfied without it? Indeed, the unrest and inward conflict, so characteristic of our universal human nature, are but the results of man's disharmony with God. Created in the image of God, with a mental and moral nature like his, nothing but God can satisfy man's highest needs. The spirit of man is too capacious—has too royal a birth—to be satisfied with what this earth can give it. The body, made from this earth, can be fed by the earth; but the soul, having come from God, can only be fed by him. Christ has brought us a fuller revelation of God than David knew, and gives new and stronger reasons why the soul should long for him. He is our Father. He so loved the world as to give his only begotten Son to save it. O the infinite depths and tenderness of His love! O the sweetness of that rest and peace which the wearied soul finds in reposing on the bosom of Christ! What plummet line can sound the depth of that compassion which utters itself in the gracious words:

"Come unto me, all ye that labor and are heavy laden, and I will give you rest." Alas, that we should go through life with our souls full of unrest, and never heed this invitation, nor perceive that it is meant for us.

Jesus is God's response to the soul's cry for the "living God." When he spoke to the woman at Jacob's well of that water which he would give, of which, if one drink, he shall never thirst, he spoke of that thirst of the soul after God of which the psalmist of Israel sang centuries before. It is, therefore, the universal need of man in all ages. How strong is the word chosen to express that need! Thirst is, perhaps, the most intense desire the human body may know. Its pangs to the thirsty traveler in the parched desert are almost insufferable. What thirst is to the body, this desire is to the human soul. O that we could realize that it is only in Christ that the soul's needs are fully met.

In that wonderful sermon of Jesus on the mount, he said: "Blessed are they that hunger and thirst after righteousness, for they shall he filled." This thirst or intense desire for righteousness is not different from the thirst for God. They are different names for the same great longing of the human soul. This desire for God and his righteousness is the mark of the soul's divine origin and kinship. It is also an unfailing sign of the normal and healthful condition of the soul. The soul that thirsts for God has come into right relations to the source of its life and being. The prodigal son for awhile felt satisfied with the gratification of the desires of his lower nature, but, when he "came to himself," he immediately thought of his father's house and how he had sinned against heaven and in his father's sight. The thoughtless and worldly-minded may become so infatuated with the world's pleasures and its wealth and honor, as to be unconscious of their need of God, and to experience no desire for communion with him. When such is the case, the soul is in captivity to Satan. It has come to that depraved condition that it loves sin, and has no appreciation of its true nature and awful consequences. It is in a state of moral insensibility. All the higher aspirations and nobler capacities are smothered by the desires of the flesh. As we deem one sick, in body, who has no appetite for healthful food, and will not partake of it, so may we regard that soul as diseased, and in an abnormal condition, that has no hunger and thirst for God, nor for his truth and righteousness.

When such a soul comes to itself, that is, resumes its normal attitude toward God, it at once begins to relish God's word, and to long for communion and fellowship with him. It will avail itself of private prayer and will not neglect the public worship of God. How sweet are the songs of Zion to a heart that thirsts for God! How helpful are the preacher's earnest words, declaring the riches of God's grace in Christ Jesus! How tender and impressive the memorial feast of the Lord's Supper! It is, in such a mood, that the soul can exclaim:

"How amiable are thy tabernacles O Lord of hosts!"
Psalm 84:1

And when, for any reason, the soul thus united to God is deprived of the privilege of public worship, the natural language is:

"My soul longeth, yea, even fainteth, for the courts of the Lord;
My heart and my flesh cry out unto the living God."
Psalm 84:2

How beautiful and inspiring a thing is public worship, when Christians meet in such a state of spiritual longing as these words express. No one could enter into such an assembly without being brought consciously nearer to God. There could be no listlessness, no yawning, no impatience to get away, no disposition to criticize the preacher's voice or gestures or rhetoric, or the music. What a luxury it would be to preach to a congregation whose souls were panting for God and thirsting for the water of life! What a prayer meeting such a church could have! O that there were more private and family devotion at home; more daily meditation on the word of God; that there might be new power and inspiration in the public worship, and more thirsting for the living God!

Prayer

Almighty God, our Heavenly Father, who did create man in your own image, with desires and needs which this world cannot satisfy, grant, I beseech you, that my soul may find rest and full satisfaction in you. I thank you for the rich revelation of your love and gracious care for man which you have given us in Jesus Christ; that in him the fullness of the Godhead did dwell bodily; that, by his death and resurrection from the dead, you have provided for man's forgiveness and for his existence beyond the grave. Yea, every need of the soul is met in Christ. In him we are complete. O that my soul may ever realize this truth and seek its happiness and its satisfaction in you. Forbid, gracious Father, that my heart should ever be won from you by the world's pleasures, honors or riches. You alone can supply the wants of my nature. Draw me closer to you, and in every storm of trial or temptation, may I find rest and refuge in you. Increase my desire for you, O God, so that my soul may find its supreme delight in communion with you. And grant that, having found your fellowship very sweet on earth, I may be permitted to spend eternity with you, for Christ's sake. Amen!

3. The Tender Shepherd

The Lord is my shepherd; I shall not want.
PSALM 23:1

So sang David, who, himself, in his boyhood, had tended his father's sheep in the wilderness not far from his native Bethlehem. The care and solicitude of an Eastern shepherd for his flock he knew from experience. He knew the dangers to which these flocks were exposed in the deep solitudes, from wild beasts, robbers and from sudden torrents. Had he not imperiled his own life in defending his father's sheep from the lion and the bear in the wilderness? (I Samuel 17:34-36). He had been called from the sheepfolds at Bethlehem to be a king and shepherd of Israel (Psalm 78:70-72). It was because he had been "faithful over a few things" that the Lord chose him to be a "ruler over many things." In the sad experiences he had with Saul, and in the anxieties and responsibilities of his kingdom, he had come to know the Lord's tender care for him, and hence was enabled to sing, out of his own heart, this idyllic psalm, which has been a solace to so many troubled hearts in all subsequent ages.

What a beautiful picture of Christ's love and care for his disciples. How tenderly the shepherd guards the young and feeble of his flock, often carrying the lambs in his bosom. So it was prophesied of Christ by Isaiah: "He shall feed his flock like a shepherd; he shall gather the lambs with his arm and carry them in his bosom; and shall gently lead those that are with young" (Isaiah 40:11). How he bears with our infirmities. "He knoweth our frame, that we are dust." What a scene of pastoral beauty and loveliness is here brought before us, with its "still waters" and "green pastures." How bountiful the provision for our soul's needs suggested by verdant fields and the deep, quiet pools. As the sheep never lies down in the green and tender grass until its wants are fully met and it is perfectly content, what a striking and beautiful picture this is of the soul's peace and contentment in Christ. Faithful and tender Shepherd that he is, he will not desert us, though we walk through the valley and shadow of death. His rod and staff will comfort us even there, so that we need fear no evil. O the precious comfort of knowing that Christ is over us continually with a shepherd's watchful eye, and that he is mighty and able to save. It is this feeling of security in divine care that inspired one of our own sweet poets to sing:

> *"I know not where his islands lift*
> *Their fronded palms in air;*
> *I only know I cannot drift*
> *Beyond his love and care."*

Prayer

O you great Shepherd of the sheep, I am one of the weakest of your flock; the more reason, therefore, have I to thank you that you have taken me under your tender care. Exposed to sin and to all the perils that Satan spreads in my way, how could I do without your strong hand to uphold me? Accept my warmest thanks, dear Lord, that when I was wandering far away from your fold, on the dark mountains of sin, exposed to eternal ruin, you did come to seek and to save me. I bless you that I have ever heard and heeded your tender voice, calling unto me and saying: "Come unto me, and I will give you rest." And now, O Lord, that I have committed myself and all my interests for time and eternity to your care, put around me the strong arm of your love, guide me with your shepherd's staff in paths of righteousness; restore my soul when it is faint and weary; deliver me from all the dangers that beset me, and when at last I am called to pass through the dark valley of the shadow of death, O gentle Shepherd, be with me in that otherwise lone passage, and comfort me when all other comforters fail. And when my eyes shall close forever on mortal scenes, grant that they may open on fairer fields and brighter visions of life eternal and "behold the King in his beauty," and I will give unceasing praise to Father, Son and Holy Spirit, world without end. Amen!

4. The Gift of the Holy Spirit

I will pray the Father and he will give you another Comforter that he may abide with you forever, even the Spirit of truth whom the world cannot receive, because it seeth him not, neither knoweth him; but ye know him, for he dwelleth with you and shall be in you.
JOHN 14:16,17

God's gifts to men are on a scale of royal munificence. He gave man his own image in his creation, and then gave him dominion over the earth and over all the infinite tenantry of life which inhabit it. All through human history God has lavished his gifts upon men, revealing himself to them as they were able to understand his revelations, and giving them the knowledge of his will. But the two greatest gifts God ever gave to men were the gift of his Son, and the gift of the Holy Spirit. Christ's mission was to reveal God as Father. The Holy Spirit's mission was to reveal Christ to his disciples and lead them to a clear understanding of the sublime significance of the incarnation and its related truths. Compare the condition of Christ's disciples before and after receiving the promised Comforter or Advocate, in order to realize the importance of the Spirit's mission. Before Pentecost they were doubtful, hesitating, still ignorant of Christ's mission, and timid. After that day they comprehended Christ's true character and mission, saw clearly the significance of his death and resurrection, and were courageous and fearless in their testimony. How incomplete would have been the scheme of human redemption without the gift of the Holy Spirit! After Christ's glorification, the Comforter came to carry on his work by illuminating the minds and strengthening the hearts of his disciples, and to be a Helper and a Comforter who should "abide forever." This settles the question as to the continuance of the Holy Spirit in the church. He is not only to "convict the world of sin, of righteousness and of judgment," but he sustains to believers the important relations of Comforter, Helper, Guide, Guest, Enlightener, Sanctifier, Strengthener and Witness, through whose gracious agency the love of God is shed abroad in the heart. In a word, it is by the Spirit that Christ fulfills his promise to his disciples that he will not leave them "desolate" but will come unto them. It was "expedient" that he should go away from them in bodily presence that he might henceforth be with them in spiritual presence to carry on his work in them.

There can be no doubt that the gift of the Holy Spirit was to be one of the chief characteristics of the Christian dispensation. Was it not this, especially, that made Christ say that the least in the kingdom of God was greater than John the Baptist? John, indeed, baptized in water, but he who came after him, who was so much greater than John that the latter deemed himself unworthy to loose his sandals, baptized in the Holy Spirit. Granted that this baptism in the Holy Spirit involved miraculous manifestations limited to the apostolic age, it yet remains true that the results of this miraculous outpouring are a permanent inheritance in the church. Of this fountain of spiritual power all believers are to partake, and by partaking, to become sources of spiritual influence. Hence, it was, that on the last, and the great day of the feast, "Jesus stood and cried, saying, If any man thirst, let him come unto me and drink. He that believeth on me, as the scripture hath said, out of his belly shall flow rivers of living water. *But this spake he of the Spirit, which they that believed on him were to receive:* for the Spirit was not yet given, because Jesus was not yet glorified" (John 7:37-39).

This remarkable passage teaches the following important truths:

1. The soul's thirst for God and for righteousness can be satisfied only by Christ.
2. Those, only, who believe on Christ, can "drink" of the living water that he supplies.
3. That "living water," of which believers in Christ may drink, and which, thenceforth, is to flow from them in streams so copious as to be called "rivers," is, as the evangelist explains, the Holy Spirit.
4. The Holy Spirit, however, at that time had not been given, in the special way mentioned by Jesus.
5. The giving of the Holy Spirit, in this way, was not to be until the glorification of Christ, and hence was limited to the Christian dispensation, beginning on Pentecost following Christ's resurrection.

These truths may well lead us to inquire whether we have availed ourselves of the crowning glory of the dispensation in which we live, and have so drunk of the Holy Spirit, through faith in Christ, as that our souls have become *fountains* of living water. Alas, how barren and unfruitful are the lives of many professed Christians! Is this not because they have failed, through unbelief, to receive the Spirit, whose life-giving power beautifies and adorns whatever it touches? If our lives be permeated by the Spirit of God, they will not fail to influence the lives with which we come in contact; and thus, by spiritual leaven, the whole unevangelized mass of mankind is to be leavened with the gospel, not only preached, by our lips, but lived in our lives. I cannot resist the solemn conviction that many among us, in their opposition to wild and visionary theories about the Spirit's methods, have gone to the opposite, and none the less harmful extreme, of neglecting to give sufficient emphasis to the proper and essential work of the Holy Spirit—source of life, comfort, peace, joy, love and unity. I would urge upon all my readers a careful re-study of this important subject, in the light of the Holy Scriptures. The spiritual nature of Christ's kingdom, compared with the fleshly rites of Judaism, is its chief and most glorious characteristic. To overlook this fact or to neglect to give it due prominence, would be to fail at a vital point.

In view of these gracious offices of the Spirit, how precious is Christ's word: "Much more will your heavenly Father give the Holy Spirit to them that ask him." O that my heart may ever be a temple of the Holy Spirit! As he brooded of old over the primitive chaos of the newly-created world, clothing it with life, order and beauty, so may he quicken and make fruitful all the latent powers and capacities of my being, and mould them in the image of Christ.

Prayer

You gracious Giver of all our gifts, how infinitely great and tender must be your love that has found expression in the unnumbered mercies that have crowned our lives. Accept the gratitude of my heart, O loving Father, for giving me a place, humble though it may be, in your great family. Hear me, while I plead for the Holy Spirit in larger measure, to enlighten, quicken, comfort and strengthen me in your service. Since we are assured by your well-beloved Son that you are willing to give your Holy Spirit to them that ask you, I would with the more boldness ask this great gift at your hand. How much I need His presence within me, that I may be strong to resist evil, that the love of God may be shed abroad in my heart, that my life may be like a fruitful garden and that my character may be conformed to your divine will! O may the fruit of the Spirit abound in me, that I may be used of you in bringing others into fellowship with you. Forbid, O God, that I should grieve your Holy Spirit, by impure thoughts, unkind words, unrighteous acts, or by a life of careless indifference to the claims of religion. Help me to remember that my body is a temple of the Holy Spirit, and to keep it pure from all defilement. Through your Spirit transform me, O God, into the image of your Son, and finally fashion this mortal body into the likeness of Christ's glorious body, that where he is there I may be also. And this I ask in his precious name. Amen!

5. Christ Our Completeness

For in him dwelleth all the fullness of the Godhead bodily, and in him we are made full, who is the head of all principality and power.

COL. 2:9, 10

The revised rendering of this striking passage, as given above, brings out a beautiful and precious thought, which is somewhat obscured in the common version. The Greek word rendered *made full* is the verb form of the same word (*pleeroma*) rendered *fullness* in the first clause, showing the apostle's meaning to be that as in Christ there dwells all the fullness of deity, in bodily form (*somatikos*), so we, likewise, by our union with Christ, are partakers of that same fullness. That is to say, every disciple of Christ, in his measure, is to be a divine incarnation—an embodiment of those graces and virtues, and of that quality of life and character which belong to God. This is a most daring and sublime thought, but it is not peculiar to Paul. Peter speaks of our becoming "partakers of the divine nature," and John, soaring in his eagle flight in the loftiest ranges of thought, declares that "when Christ is manifested we shall be like him, for we shall see him as he is"—a vision possible only to the "pure in heart."

No fact forces itself more frequently or painfully on our observation and consciousness than the imperfect and fragmentary character of our lives. Whether we consider the inadequacy of our knowledge of the greatest truths and problems in the universe, our inability to recognize at all times the reality of the spiritual world, or our unsatisfactory efforts to live up to our ideals of life, we see only that which is partial, incomplete and imperfect. Not only do we "know in part and prophesy in part," but as a consequence, we *live* only "in part." The affections of the heart, no less than the intellections of the mind, are fragmentary. And yet this apostle, who reminds us of the incompleteness of our earthly life, is the same one that tells us of the completeness, fullness and rotundity of our lives in Christ. In him this inspired man of God sees the remedy for all our imperfections and incompleteness, because "in him dwelleth the fullness of the Godhead, bodily." This incarnation of divine fullness was for the purpose of communicating it to human need. Hence John tells us that Christ was "full of grace and truth" and that "of his fullness have all we received, and grace for grace" (John 1:14, 16).

In another significant passage, Paul analyzes this divine sufficiency in Christ as a prism separates a ray of white light into its constituent colors. He says that Christ is "made unto us wisdom from God, and righteousness, and sanctification, and redemption" (I Cor. 1:30). As "wisdom from God," Christ supplements all our intellectual deficiencies. What folly to turn away from Christ, the "wisdom from God," to learn from modern savants of science, concerning the great problems of life and death! As our "righteousness," all our sins find pardon in his infinite mercy and our depraved hearts find renewal in his redeeming grace. As our "sanctification," the "law of the spirit of life" in him frees us from "the law of sin and death," (Rom.

8:2) strengthens our weakness, and conforms us into his image from one degree of glory to another. As our "redemption," he shall "fashion anew the body of our humiliation, that it may be conformed to the body of his glory, according to the working whereby he is able to subject all things to himself" (Phil. 3:21).

Is there *any* want of our nature that is not provided for in Christ? What proof, convincing and overwhelming, is this, that the author of Christianity is the author of man! O the folly of turning away from Christ, who is the perfection and fullness of our being, to "philosophy and vain deceit, after the tradition of men, after the rudiments of the world!" To recognize in him one who is able to harmonize all the contradictions of our nature and to round out into completeness all the deficiencies of our lives, is the fundamental condition of all true and right living. This is why faith in him is the primal law of spiritual renewal, and the confession of him, in this unique relation, was made the foundation of his church. One who had caught a glimpse of Christ, in this beneficent aspect of his relations to humanity, exclaimed: "For you, therefore, who believe, is the preciousness" (1 Pet. 2:7). That is, faith is the channel by which the blessings in Christ are conveyed to men. It is unbelief, both in church members and in non-church members, that impoverishes souls, and deprives them of the riches of God's grace in Christ. Once the soul, hungering and thirsting after righteousness, sees in Christ the fulfillment of all its holiest desires and aspirations, he becomes "the chiefest among ten thousand," and "altogether lovely" (Song of Solomon 5:10-16). This apprehension of Christ makes communion with him, instead of an irksome duty, a constant delight and a source of unfailing joy.

But why, since we are "made full" in Christ, and all our emptiness of soul is provided for in his infinite fullness, do we who believe, experience, so often, the consciousness of spiritual leanness, and of weakness in the presence of temptation? Why must we often say, with the psalmist: "Why art thou cast down, O my soul, and why are thou disquieted within me?" (Psalm 43:5). The answer to these questions is to be found in the fact that our possession of, and full participation in, this fullness of Christ, is a process which advances towards completion according to the law of spiritual growth. Here, as everywhere else in God's great universe, it is "first the blade, then the ear, then the full corn in the ear" (Mark 4:28). Those who expect by one bound to spring into the perfection of Christian character, and the fullness of spiritual life and blessing, have not learned God's method. These provisions for all our needs, in Christ, are indeed regarded as ours, because intended for our use, but they must be appropriated by faith, and made our own subjectively, through the process of sanctification. He who would find complete soul-rest in Christ, must *take his yoke* and *learn of him* (Matt. 11:28, 29)—meaning entire subjection to his will in all things. This involves sacrifices which many are unwilling to make. Hence, the low plane of spiritual life on which so many of us are content to live.

There is no evil that I feel more inclined to warn my young Christian readers against, than the setting up of a low standard of Christian life. Once the glowing and radiant example of Christ is lost sight of, and we settle down into a stereotyped mediocrity between ungodliness and sainthood, Christianity loses all its inspiration. No great and heroic characters are formed under this conception of Christian life. It breeds Pharisees, but creates no material for martyrdom. It generates no lofty enthusiasm, such as we see in Paul and John and other great heroes of faith. It may be zealous of its tithes of anise, mint and cumin, but it has no taste or capacity for dealing with the weightier problems of saving the outcasts, relieving human misery, evangelizing the world and elevating the race. Men must feel the heartthrobs of Christ in their own bosoms, and enter into profound sympathy with his thought and life, to undertake, successfully, these great tasks of life. Thus, it is seen, how closely connected are individual progress in godliness and the general advancement of Christ's kingdom in the world.

In view of these considerations, it is pertinent to ask whether God, having made such ample provision for our growth and perfection, will hold us guiltless if we fail to make the most of our opportunities and develop the highest possible type of character? Are we not under the same obligations to reach the highest possible mark in Christian attainment that we are under to be Christians at all? So it seems to us.

O that all who read these pages may inwardly resolve, God helping them, to avail themselves more fully of the infinite treasures of truth and grace in Christ, that, so filled with all the fullness of God, they may reach forth strong and helpful hands to those who are struggling with the adverse currents of evil, and are going down in the dark waters of sin! And may the fullness of grace and truth wherewith Christ hath blessed us, flow out, in life-giving streams, to the barren wastes of other lives and make them as fruitful gardens of the Lord!

Prayer

Our Father, who is in heaven, how great is the love which you have shown to the children of men! Not only did you so love the world as to give your only begotten Son to redeem it from sin, but in him you have made provision for all our manifold needs. You did make him unto us wisdom, righteousness, sanctification and redemption. Forbid, Almighty God, that I should despise the riches of your grace, or be satisfied with my present attainments in Christian knowledge and character. Grant unto me, and unto all your children, according to the riches of your glory, that we may be strengthened with power through your Spirit in the inward man; that Christ may dwell in our hearts through faith; to the end that we, being rooted and grounded in love, may be strong to apprehend, with all the saints, what is the breadth and length and height and depth, and to know the love of Christ, which passes knowledge, that we maybe filled with all the fullness of God. And now, unto him that is able to do exceeding abundantly above all that we ask or think, according to the power that works in us, unto him be glory in the church, and in Christ Jesus, unto all generations forever and ever. Amen!

6. In God's Image

And God said, Let us make man in our image, after our likeness; and let them have dominion over the fish of the sea and the fowl of the air and over the cattle, and over all the earth, and over every creeping thing that creepeth upon the earth. And God created man in his own image, in the image of God created he him; male and female created he them.   GEN. 1: 26, 27

What a stupendous fact! Man created in the image of God! How few seem to grasp its significance. What light it throws on the great problems of human life. What a wide chasm it makes between man and all lower orders of created being. Here is a basal fact without which there can be no true theology or anthropology. Surely, here is sacred ground. Let us remove the sandals from our feet while we meditate reverently on the meaning of this marvelous truth. With bowed heads, let us invoke the guidance of the Holy Spirit while we seek to understand the lesson contained in these wonderful words.

"Let us make man in our image, after our likeness." This is the divine counsel and purpose that lie back of the great mystery of human life and all its pages of tragic history. It is a purpose formed deliberately and in full view of all its mighty consequences—sin, suffering, sorrow, conflict, death, the incarnation, Gethsemane, Calvary, the open Sepulchre, redemption! "God is love." Out of all this struggle, discord and misery, then, there are to flow results that will more than vindicate the wisdom and goodness of God. Let this sweet reflection comfort our hearts until life's conflicts shall issue in eternal peace.

"And God created man in his own image." Is it possible for the human mind to reach the pinnacle of thought that these words suggest? Not now; but let us pause reverently before them and seek a nearer approach to their full meaning. It cannot be that in his bodily or fleshly nature man is created in God's image, for God is spirit. The human body is not man, nor any essential part of man. The man exists when his body returns to dust whence it came. It is the condition of man's earthly existence. It is the house of clay in which the real man dwells for the time. What, then, is the real man which no mortal eye hath ever seen? Is it not the conscious, intelligent ego, that which thinks, chooses, apprehends moral motives, discerns between right and wrong and determines what motives shall influence its action? If so, then man is created in God's image, (1) intellectually, (2) morally, (3) volitionally. The proof of this is supplied in every man's own consciousness, in connection with God's written revelation of his will and character.

1. That man is created in God's image in his mental constitution is evidenced by the fact that he can "think God's thoughts after him," as Kepler has so finely said. God's thoughts are manifest in all the arrangements of the material universe. Everywhere there is plan, method, adaptation, design—the manifestations of the divine mind. Man can see, appreciate and make practical use of these thoughts of God. If his mind were not in the image of God, this would not be

possible. God reasons with men and communicates his will to them on the basis of this likeness. Of what use could the Ten Commandments be to a tribe of chattering apes, or a village of prairie dogs? God cannot convey such truths to these lower orders of creation, because there is nothing in their nature to apprehend such thoughts. A man can convey thoughts to the mind of his prattling child that can by no means be conveyed to the most sagacious of beasts, because the child is in his own mental image and the beast is not. There are, of course, thoughts that we cannot communicate to the undeveloped mind of our children, just as there are truths that God cannot reveal to the greatest intellects on earth, because they are not yet able to receive them. Likeness does not imply equality, but it does open up possibilities of limitless progress.

2.   The proof that man's moral nature is after the pattern of God's, may be found in the fact that man approves the moral law of God, however much he may violate it. Nor does he wait until some future judgment for an accuser. His own conscience—God's vicegerent in the human breast, as someone has called it—the reflection of God's moral nature within man—is his accuser. With the majesty and authority of a supreme judge, it passes sentence on us when we violate that law and approves us when we yield obedience to it. When God says, "thou shalt not steal," "thou shalt not bear false witness," "thou shalt not murder," etc., man's moral nature approves these expressions of the eternal law of right. If man's moral nature were unlike that of God, this would not be the case. In that event, a man might violate the moral law of God while acting in perfect harmony with the moral law of his own nature. This would destroy all idea of personal accountability, and render a judgment day impossible. The basis of man's accountability to God is the likeness of his moral nature to that of God.

But if man be created in the moral image of God, marred though that image be by sin, what glorious possibilities of righteousness and holiness are open before him, and what fearful responsibility rests on him who debauches that nature.

3. That man is endowed with *will*, and has the power of *choosing*, is at once his crown of glory and his chief danger. God wills and it is done. His will is the law of the universe. When he made man in his own image, he clothed him with the sublime and fearful prerogative of determining his own destiny, of choosing between motives. Confused with the subtle discussions of the schoolmen about "free will and necessity," we turn to our own consciousness as a witness, and it testifies that every day and every hour, of our conscious existence, we are choosing between motives and deciding between this and that course of action. And when under the blinding influence of passion, appetite or ambition, we yield to the lower instead of the higher motive, no plausible fallacy about the necessity that controlled our action suffices to protect us against the accusations of our conscience. We feel and recognize our *guilt*. We *had* the power to choose otherwise and we *know* it, else there would be no consciousness of guilt. All this is assumed, too, in the provisions that God has made for man's salvation. As sin is a matter of choice, so is salvation. God saves no man against his will. *"Choose* ye this day whom ye will serve," is his command in all times and to all peoples. Christ does not cross the threshold of man's volition uninvited. "Behold, I stand at the door and knock. *If any man hear my voice and open the door*, I will come in to him, and will sup with him and he with me" (Rev. 3: 21).

Here, then, is the solution of the dark problem of the origin of sin, so far as it is given us to know it. It is the abuse of freedom—of the power of choice. Here, too, is the great underlying reason of the incarnation and of the cross. The world must have a more perfect representation of God than the sinning race exhibited. Christ came as "the effulgence of his glory and the very image of his substance" (Heb. 1: 3). Man, a moral being, and a free, self-determining agent, must be won to God by moral motives. The stubborn will must be conquered by supreme love. Hence Gethsemane and Calvary. Why did not God save man by his naked omnipotence, without the awful tragedy of the cross? Because God created man in his own image, and such a being must be wooed and won by love, not driven by force.

In the light of these truths, I can answer the question asked by David, who, on surveying the magnitude of the material universe, was led to inquire,

> "What is man that thou are mindful of him, and the Son of man that thou visitest him?"   Psalm 8:4

What is he? He is God's child in his own image. That is why he is mindful of him, and why he has visited him in the person of Jesus Christ. My own parental heart teaches me why God would spare no effort to save his lost and erring children. O how this magnifies the cross and honors man!

O my soul, consider well your high origin, the image which you wear, and weigh the responsibilities which come with such high endowments. Here, in the hush of this solemn stillness, alone with God, let me hear your loving voice, dear Savior, and open the door of my heart and let you in, that I may sup with you and you with me!

Prayer

Almighty God, our most gracious heavenly Father, when I consider with what powers and capacities you did endow your creature, man, and for what high and holy service you have qualified him, I am filled with shame and confusion at the remembrance of all my sins and short-comings. I confess before you, my transgressions, and all my faults and frailties, and beseech you, in the name of your well-beloved Son, to grant me your pardoning mercy and sustaining grace. I thank you for all my bodily and mental faculties, and especially for that moral nature which most allies me to you, and which I have so much abused. I bless your holy name that you did pity us, in our fallen condition, and send us your only begotten Son, full of grace and truth, through whom we regain fellowship with you, have our sinful nature renewed, and enter into your most blessed service. And O God, be pleased to so quicken me by your Spirit, and uphold me, by your right hand, that I may fill the purpose for which you have created me. Help me to use diligently all the means of grace which you have provided, and so grow continually both in grace and in the knowledge of the truth. Enable me to see the folly and the emptiness of all earthly allurements that would draw me away from you. Help me to understand more fully that, created as I am in your image, you alone can satisfy the needs of my soul. May this thought, of the dignity and worth of a human soul not only lead me to more earnest efforts for my own salvation, but may it give me far greater concern for the salvation of others. O you blessed Savior, who did stoop from heaven to earth, and did drink the bitter cup of death, for sinful and lost humanity, imbue me with more of your spirit, that I may be willing to enter into the fellowship of your sufferings and do all in my power for the salvation of my fellow-men! And finally, O Father, when we have finished the work you have given us to do, and it seems good to you to call us home, give us, we beseech you, an abundant entrance into your everlasting kingdom through Jesus Christ our Lord. Amen!

.

7. Coming to God

For he that cometh to God must believe that he is, and that he is a rewarder of them that seek after him.   HEB. 11: 6

Coming to God! What a privilege! What a door of opportunity! If we had access to earth's greatest and wisest men, who, at any hour, on any day, would hear our trouble and perplexity, and give us their sympathetic counsel and help, would we not very highly prize it? If Gabriel and Michael, princes of heaven, should declare themselves accessible to all of the struggling, tempted, and suffering ones of earth, at any time, and should signify their willingness to enlist themselves in our behalf, with all their angelic power, and superhuman strength, would there be many who, knowing this fact, would be insensible to the advantage thus placed within their reach and neglect to avail themselves of it? It is only by such gradations that the human mind can rise to the height of the great privilege of going to the great and infinite God with all our cares and needs, assured of his willingness to hear and to answer us in mercy. Perhaps the strangest moral phenomenon on earth is the general neglect of this royal privilege of prayer, in Christian lands and even in Christian churches.

What would be thought of a young man, who, having a father of abundant means, who loved his children tenderly and delighted in conferring favors upon them, should be found on the streets of a strange city without money, food or decent apparel, begging a crust of bread from door to door? "Fool! " men would say who knew the circumstances; "why does he not go to his father who is so able and anxious to help him?" But would such a course be any more strange or unreasonable, than that pursued by many professed Christians, who, in spiritual poverty and weakness, in heart-hunger and soul-weariness, go anywhere and everywhere else for relief, rather than to their heavenly Father, who loves to give good things to his children? There is only one explanation of the strange fact; unbelief has blinded the heart of such, so that they neither realize their spiritual need, nor the personal presence and gracious character of God.

In the passage quoted above two conditions are mentioned as essential to coming to God, or to prayer, which is coming to God in its highest and holiest sense, namely: 1. Belief in the existence of a personal God; 2. Belief in his gracious character as a Rewarder of those who seek him. These conditions are grounded in the very nature of prayer. Prayer is communion with God. It is going to God with all our needs. "It is," as one writer has said, "helplessness casting itself on power. It is infirmity leaning on strength, and misery wooing bliss. It is unholiness embracing purity, and hatred desiring love. It is corruption panting for immortality, and earth-borns claiming kindred in the skies. It is the flight of the soul to the bosom of God, and the spirit soaring upward and claiming nativity beyond the stars. It is the restless dove on drooping wing, turned to its loved repose. It is the soaring eagle mounting upward in its flight, and with steady gaze pursuing the track till lost to all below. It is the roving wanderer looking towards his abiding place, where are all his treasures and his gold. It is the prisoner pleading for release. It is the mariner of a dangerous sea, upon the reeling topmast, descrying the broad and quiet haven of repose. It is the soul, oppressed by earthly soarings, escaping to a broader and purer sphere, and bathing its plumes in the ethereal and eternal." Aye, it is the immortal spirit, having become conscious of its divine origin, turning to God for the deep satisfactions which the earth cannot give.

How can such a state or action of the soul exist in the absence of true faith, the realization of the existence, personal presence and gracious character of God? On the vividness and power of such realization, the value and joy of prayer depend. This fact is an explanation of much of the joylessness and unsatisfactoriness in prayer, of which many complain, and which all of us, at times, have experienced. We sometimes rush into the presence of God, through the form of prayer, without suitable preparation for so holy an exercise. We have given no time to meditation or to self-examination. We have been too slothful, mentally, to make an effort to fix in our minds, clearly, the great essential truths on which prayer is based: God is. He is a Person. He is here. He has promised to hear me when I call on him. He cannot lie. He loves to give good gifts to his needy children. He has heard and answered prayer. He has answered my prayers. He has invited me to ask him for what I need. Let the eye of faith rest on these basal truths, and let the mind revolve them, until they carry clearness of conviction to the heart. Then let the soul look in on its own poverty until there is a clear apprehension of its needs. Let the voice of conscience be heard, in this still hour, that there may be contrition for past sins. Let past mercies and answers to prayer be remembered that there may be thankfulness, and an assured conviction of the value of prayer. From such meditations the soul mounts up to God in prayer, as the lark rises from the meadow grass and soars joyfully towards the sun, singing as it soars.

No one would think of going into the presence of an earthly king or potentate, to seek a favor, without proper preparation of his apparel, and a clear and distinct understanding of the request he was to make. Do we not ofttimes treat God with less respect, carrying into his presence sins unrepented of, hearts ungrateful for his daily mercies and minds preoccupied with worldly thoughts and cares, having only a vague and indistinct idea of the favors we need? True, he does not spurn us from his presence as an earthly monarch would do, because he knows our frame and remembers that we are dust, yet, by an eternal law as unchangeable as God, we are hindered from receiving the blessing we need, because of our lack of preparation for receiving it.

To believe that God is a Rewarder of them that seek after him is to believe in prayer as a positive spiritual force in the universe. A modern theory of prayer, held by some good people, to the effect that its influence is wholly subjective, that it is a sort of spiritual exercise which makes people better, but that it in no way affects God, is doing much, we fear, to sap the foundation of prayer and of personal piety. This is not the scriptural view of prayer. Above all, it is not in harmony with Christ's teaching on the subject of prayer. With him prayer is something more than pious reverie. It is asking God for what we need, an intensely practical thing. The examples of prayer given in the Bible all confirm this view of it. Prayer is, indeed, a lofty exercise of the soul, when regarded as communion of the soul with a personal God, who deigns to hear our cries, and its influence on the mind and heart cannot but be exalting and purifying. In no other act does the soul assert its divine paternity so clearly as in seeking communion with and blessings from the Father of Spirits, But the value, the dignity, and the power of prayer grow out of the fact, that it is the cry of a human soul uttered in the ear of the Almighty Father, who will withhold no good thing from them that walk uprightly.

This subjective and defective view of prayer that limits its influence to the petitioner rests on the idea that a contrary theory involves the changeableness of God, and the instability of divine law. But is not this a superficial view of the subject? What if prayer be a divine force, ordained of God and having its legitimate place in the order of the universe? As another has expressed it, "prayer has, and God has determined that it should have, a positive and appreciable influence in directing the course of a human life. It is, and God has purposed that it should be, a link of connection between human mind and divine mind, by which, through his infinite condescension, we may actually move His will. It is, and God has decreed that it should be, a power in the universe, as distinct, as real, as natural and as uniform, as the power of gravitation, or of light, or of electricity. A man may use it as trustingly and as soberly as he would use either of these. It is as truly the dictate of good sense that a man should expect to achieve something by praying, as it is that he should expect to achieve something by a telescope or the mariner's compass, or the electric telegraph. "

With such views of God as a Rewarder, and of prayer as a force ordained by him to connect human needs with divine resources, we may "draw near with boldness unto the throne of grace, that we may receive mercy, and may find grace to help us in time of need." (Heb 4:16) Thanks be unto God that there is a way of approach to him through the blood of the everlasting covenant!

Prayer

Almighty God, Our Heavenly Father, I do believe, not only that you are, but that you are a Rewarder of them that diligently seek you, and hunger and thirst after your righteousness. Therefore do I come to you. Not because I am pure and strong and whole in every part, and can approach unto you with a perfect heart and a perfect utterance, do I come, but because I am sinful, weak and wounded by Satan, and feel my need of you. O Father, you will not despise our petitions, if they be inadequately expressed, for the Holy Spirit does help our infirmities, making intercession for us with groanings which cannot be uttered in words of human speech. I thank you, O God, that I can come to you with humble boldness through the mediation of Jesus Christ, and feel that you are my Father, and that You love me with a depth of tenderness and compassion, which passes knowledge. In my shortsightedness, I do not always know what is best for me, but you know, dear Father, and to you I commit myself. Your will be done in me, through me and with me. I am blind, and come to you for sight; weak, and come to you for strength; sinful, and come to you for cleansing; weary of the world's strife, and come to you for rest; assailed by trials and temptations, both from within and without, I come to you for refuge, for you, O Lord, are my Rock, my Fortress and my Defense, in every danger and in every trouble. O will you receive me, loving Father, through the merits of Jesus Christ, your Son, and put your everlasting arms about me and give me peace. By the moral beauty and the infinite compassion of Jesus, may the whole world be drawn into your loving embrace, that righteousness and peace may reign, triumphant, over all the earth, and your kingdom come in its fullness of power and blessing, and your will be done on earth even as it is done in heaven. And when this mortal life is ended, we beseech you, gracious Father, that we may behold you with open vision, and dwell with you forever, through Jesus Christ, Our Lord. Amen!

8. Life's Purpose, Plan and Prize

"Brethren, I count not myself yet to have apprehended: but one thing I do, forgetting the things which are behind, and stretching forward to the things which are before, I press on toward the goal unto the prize of the high calling of God in Christ Jesus." PHIL. 3: 13-14

In this passage, the great apostle lays bare the secret of his wonderful life, by revealing its purpose, its plan, and the prize that constituted its motive power. It is a profitable thing to come into contact with a great character like Paul, whose life has so greatly influenced the life and thought of the world, and to study the secret of his wonderful power. It is for this reason that I invite the reader to a meditation, with me, on the above passage. Especially do I desire my young readers to study with me this pregnant utterance of one of the earth's greatest heroes.

Let it be noted, first of all, that this most famous preacher and theologian of the First Century, did not claim to have reached the goal of Christian perfection. He was still pressing on toward the mark. Alas for the man who imagines he has reached the limit of human progress, and that there are no unattained heights above him! How unlike Paul such a one must feel and think!

Singleness of aim was one of the factors that made Paul's life the masterful force it was in the world. All men who hope to attain large success and usefulness in Christian life must be able to say with this hero of the cross, "This one thing I do." There is only one vocation in life, though there be many avocations which men may honestly pursue in order to "provide things honest in the sight of all men." The real vocation is as high above these as the heavens are above the earth. There is no true life that finds its highest aim in an earthly pursuit, no matter how honorable or praiseworthy it may be, in itself considered. To be a lawyer, a doctor, a merchant, a farmer, a mechanic, an artist, a scientist, simply, is to miss the real aim of life. These are but means to a higher end and aim, to everyone who has come to know the meaning of life. That only worthy vocation is the attainment of God's ideal personhood, the only aim worthy of man's origin and nature. This purpose is expressed by Paul in the words *pressing on to the goal.* Just as the Grecian runner, divesting himself of all impediments, and putting aside all other aims, pressed on to the mark, and the crown at the end of the race, with all his concentrated power and energy, so he determined, leaving behind him former aims and ambitions, to center all his efforts on the one grand life-task of attaining to the divine standard of life and character as given in Jesus Christ. This alone is the terminus of the Christian race. The goal of all worthy human struggle is the attainment of the likeness of Jesus Christ. The artist who succeeds in placing on the canvas a sublime or beautiful conception, has not wrought in vain; but it is not to be compared with an achievement like that which Paul had in view.

But an aim so high as this is not to be realized without a plan, which cuts off all contrary or impeding aims and ends, and concentrates all possible power on the one true aim. Such a plan was that of Paul, "forgetting the things which are behind and stretching forward to the things which are before." He realized that the consummation of so sublime a purpose, involved the renunciation of certain things which many are unwilling to surrender, even for so great a prize as that which he had in view. This plan involves among other things the following:

1. The complete mastery of the lower nature. "I buffet my body, and bring it into bondage," (I Cor. 9:27) says Paul; and here is a conflict worthy of the metal of earth's bravest, truest, and manliest men. Here is heroism of the noblest type. He who fails here loses life's battle. How complete was the self-mastery of Jesus! How obedient were all the desires and appetites of his bodily nature to the imperious behests of his will! When we consider the dominancy of fleshly desires and appetites among the young men of this age, there is no need to wonder that there are not more Pauls, more heroes of faith. So few are willing to crucify the lusts of the flesh for the sake of spiritual gain!

2. It involves the renunciation of self, and the giving forth of all one's powers for the welfare of others. What else can Christ mean when he declares, " If any man would come after me, let him deny himself, and take up his cross, and follow me?" He who lives for self has not yet learned the alphabet of Christianity. What an all-controlling influence, then, must the fact of real discipleship of Christ exert over the whole area of one's life, in all its aims and activities. Christ enthroned in the heart must be the regnant force of our lives, if we are indeed his disciples.

3. And this leads us to say that Paul's plan of life will lead us to conform all our life-plans to the divine will. One of the problems that confront every young man sooner or later, is

"What shall be my calling or pursuit in life?" This is a very serious question and one that can be answered, satisfactorily, only in the light of our relationship to Christ. And yet it is to be feared that many young Christians choose their life work without special reference to the claims that Christ has upon their redeemed lives. A young disciple is bound to ask with Paul, "Lord, what wilt you have me to do?" He cannot but ask himself, "What help does humanity most need that I can render?" "What can I do that will help most in advancing Christ's reign upon earth?" These questions, honestly asked and prayerfully considered at the threshold of a Christian life, cannot but exert a wonderful influence over one's whole afterlife and character. They would shatter many life-plans formed on the basis of selfish motives, and dispel many an illusory dream of earthly glory to give, in its stead, at last, a vision of heavenly glory. As the Master himself turned away from tempting offers of the world's power and wealth and honor to walk the lowly path of self denial, that he might the better serve humanity, so his disciples must needs often refuse the prizes which Satan offers in order to walk with their Master in the path of unselfish service to the race. But as Christ, because of his voluntary humiliation for our sakes, was highly exalted, and given a name that is above every name, so his disciples, who suffer with him now, shall, at his coming, reign with him in glory.

4. This "stretching forward to the things which are before" involves endless progress. Christ is the goal. His perfect, sinless character, is the mark towards which we are pressing. Such an aim and such a plan of life necessitate constant growth both in grace and in the knowledge of our Lord Jesus Christ. It forbids that we should rest, contentedly, on a low plane of spiritual attainment. What an enchanting view of

life does Christianity thus present to the young! It is not a system of dead forms and arbitrary rules, but a glorious life of unending progress in knowledge and virtue, with Christ as our leader and our goal. No one who has ever caught this Christ-idea of life, ever asked the impious and audacious question, "Is life worth living?" To such a one, life is full of inspiration and incentive to high endeavor. O young people of America, and of the closing decade of the nineteenth century, Christ calls you to the highest tasks and the noblest service which ever engaged the thought and the energy of mortals.

> *"All around us, fair with flowers,*
> *Fields of beauty sleeping lie;*
> *All around us clarion voices,*
> *Call to duty stern and high."*

But Paul's life not only had its purpose and its plan; it had its prize also, "the prize of the high calling of God in Christ Jesus." It was the joy that was set before Christ that enabled him to endure the cross, despising the shame. It was the prize at the end of life's race that consoled the heart of this great apostle in the midst of his earthly losses. He "reckoned" that the sufferings of this present time "are not worthy to be compared with the glory which shall be revealed to usward," (Rom. 8:18) and had learned the divine philosophy that "Our light affliction, which is for the moment, worketh for us more and more exceedingly an eternal weight of glory." (II Cor. 4:17)

The prize of the Christian calling can be nothing less than the complete transformation into Christ's likeness, both in moral and bodily perfection, and the consequent entrance into all the blessedness of state and being which make heaven. How all the world's most coveted prizes dwindle into utter worthlessness when compared with this! It was because Paul's faith made *real* to him such a magnificent reward of Christian toil and sacrifice, that his career was filled with those heroic deeds that have made it a beacon light to all succeeding generations.

Here, in the solemn hush of this quiet hour, alone with God, dear reader, I would have you, on bended knee, adopt Paul's purpose and plan of life, and henceforth, with the divine aid, press toward the true goal of life, in Christ-like service to humanity, until the "prize of the high calling " shall be awarded you by the hand of the glorified Christ. To him be glory and dominion both now and forever. Amen!

Prayer

Our Father who is in heaven, I thank you for sending your Son into this world to show us your character and will, and to reveal to us the value and meaning of life. I thank you that by his gospel I have been led to become his disciple. O how great is my indebtedness to you, blessed Lord, for the lessons I have learned at your feet, and the rest I have found in wearing your yoke. And yet, I realize now that I have been following you at too great a distance. I have not had sufficiently at heart the great law of discipleship that you have laid down. I have served my own selfish desires too much, and have not yielded myself wholly to you to do your will. Forgive my sins and my neglect, and here and now, help me to dedicate myself anew to your service. Take from me, dear Father, all false aims in life, and all unworthy ambitions, and make me willing to do your bidding and serve you in whatever way I can do most good in the world. May I never lose sight of the true goal of life, but press forward continually towards it, giving up the dead past, and living for the things that are before, until I win the prize and am permitted to wear the crown of righteousness. I pray, O Lord of the harvest, that other lives which you have redeemed, may be consecrated to your service until a mighty host shall be marshaled for the advancement of your kingdom. Hear my prayer, gracious Father, accept my offered service, ever guide me in paths of usefulness and bring me at last, through Jesus Christ, into the service of your upper sanctuary, where we shall praise you forever. Amen!

9. The Benefit of Prayer

"What is the Almighty that we should serve him? And what profit should we have if we pray unto him?" JOB 21:15

These were the questions of the skeptics in Job's day, and they are the questions of the skeptics in our own day. It is not related that any of Job's unbelieving contemporaries ever proposed a prayer test, in order to demonstrate its futility, but that is doubtless owing to the fact that the scientific spirit was not so strongly developed in Job's day as it is in ours. It is characteristic of skepticism to doubt or deny the efficacy of prayer, just as it is characteristic of faith to affirm and illustrate its value. The two questions asked in the above quotation from Job have a very close and vital connection. Our belief concerning the Almighty, as to who, and what kind of Being he is, will determine our estimate of the value of prayer. If the Almighty be only the sum of all things, an impersonal Force that moves the Universe, then prayer is indeed meaningless. But if he be a Personal God, the Father of Our spirits, who is deeply concerned in our welfare, and who has revealed himself as a God who hears and answers prayer, then, prayer has infinite value. In this chapter, I must assume my readers to believe in the existence of such a God.

Prayer implies the existence of a personal God and man's personal responsibility to him, and can have no meaning, therefore, to unbelief. But all the great saints of the Bible, and of the annals of Christian history, have been mighty in prayer. Abraham, Jacob, Moses, Joshua, Samuel, David, Elijah, Elisha, Daniel, Hannah, Anna, Paul, and the other Apostles, and a host of mighty men since their day were all characterized by their belief in the power of prayer, and by their prayers. The most conspicuous example, however, of the value and might of prayer, both in his teaching and practice, is our Savior. Often he spent the whole night in prayer, communing with his Father, sometimes alone, at other times accompanied by a few of his most trusted disciples. Leaving the busy streets, or dismissing the thronging multitude, at eventide, he was accustomed to go into the mountain solitude, apart from the gaze of the curious, and pour out his troubled soul in the ear of the infinite and all-loving Father. It was on such an occasion, while praying on the mountain top, with Peter, James and John, that he was transfigured before them, a most significant and suggestive fact, indicating that prayer is that attitude of the soul toward God, in which he has chosen to communicate his transfiguring grace and glory to men.

When Jesus, by his example and teaching, had impressed his disciples with the value of prayer, they besought him to teach them how to pray. In answer to this request, he gave them some important rules and a form of prayer. In the face of such facts as these, what do all the objections which skeptics have urged against prayer amount to? What do I care for all that the Voltaires, Paines and Ingersolls of the world may say against the philosophy or practical utility of prayer, when

Jesus prayed constantly, and taught his disciples to pray? Did not Christ come from the bosom of the Father, and is he not higher authority on the value and nature of prayer than the combined wisdom of all the skeptical philosophers of the world? We may, therefore, dismiss at once, as unworthy of serious consideration all the objections which have been urged against prayer, on scientific or rationalistic grounds, and address ourselves to the consideration of the benefits to be derived from it.

In the first place it should be understood that prayer is not only commanded by the highest authority, and commended by the highest examples, but it is rooted and grounded in man's moral and religious nature. It is impossible to conceive of the exercise of man's religious nature without prayer, in some of its elements, as invocation, supplication, intercession and thanksgiving. But why should man have a religious nature if it is to find no natural expression? Prayer, then, is essential to the integrity of man's constitution as a moral and religious being. To oppose it, therefore, is to make war on human nature as well as on a divine ordinance, and to neglect it is to slight both a supreme duty and a royal privilege.

In attempting to enumerate the blessings that come to us through prayer, one is at a loss to decide where to begin or to end the catalogue. The best that can be done is to offer a few generalizations, and leave each individual reader to fill up the outline from his own experience. Let us consider prayer then in a few of its more important aspects.

1. *As a means of spiritual growth.* By spiritual growth I mean the development of the religious nature—the increase of faith, hope and love, of patience, purity of heart and moral strength. The relation of prayer to all these elements of Christian character is obvious. They are of heavenly implantation in the

heart, through the agency of the Holy Spirit. But our Savior taught his disciples that the Holy Spirit is given by his Father to those that ask him, saying, "If ye then, being evil, know how to give good gifts unto your children, how much more shall your heavenly Father give the Holy Spirit to them that ask him." (Luke 11:13) Here all "good gifts" seem to be summed up, by Christ, in the Holy Spirit, through whose tender brooding over the human heart, all beautiful graces and holy purposes grow into strength and vigor. Prayer is that exercise of the soul by which it tries its wings in the upper air and seeks acquaintanceship with God. Under its holy influence, all that is truest and noblest in human nature is quickened into new life and power. "Prayer has a subjective value. It is necessary to individual piety, produces solemnity, enlightens and quickens the conscience, teaches dependence, gives true views of God, and produces such a change in us as renders it consistent for him to change his course toward us."

2. *As a means of forgiveness.* The adaptation of prayer to our human nature is seen in the fact, that, although Christians, while in the flesh we are liable to sin, and that God has ordained prayer and confession of our sin, as the means of obtaining forgiveness. There is no other posture of the soul that fits it to be the recipient of forgiveness, but that of prayer. To pray truly and sincerely for forgiveness, is to be penitent for the sin we have committed, to feel, in some measure, the enormity of our guilt, and to submit ourselves, once more, to the divine government. This condition of the soul can only find expression in prayer. Who that realizes how our unforgiven sins separate us from God, and hinder communion with him, can fail, then, to appreciate the value of prayer, by which eve I receive mercy and find grace to help in time of need?" (Heb. 4:16)

3. *As a means of supplying our needs.* A prominent feature in prayer is petition, or asking God for the things that we need. Nor do the scriptures put any limit on these petitions, as our weak faith often does, shutting us up simply to spiritual blessings, and leaving out that large section of our lives which has material needs and necessities. God has respect to our temporal as well as to our spiritual needs.

He has taught us to pray for our daily food. If a businessman reaches a crisis where a certain amount of money is necessary to save his business from wreck, let him not hesitate to ask God in some way to grant him the favor, if the business is such that he is sure it meets the divine approval. Many a pious man can testify that he has found God's promise to hold good in temporal matters as well as in things spiritual. We are not to make the mistake, however, of placing as much value on these temporal gifts as upon spiritual blessings. Nor can we always feel as sure that the temporal gift we ask is best for us, as when we ask for spiritual blessings, but it is right to make our requests, subject to the will of God. But what a blessed boon it is, that in every emergency of our lives, it is our privilege to ask help from God: in sickness, to ask for health; in danger, to ask for protection; in temptation and trial, to ask for strength; in moments of perplexity and doubt, to ask for wisdom and guidance.

4. *As a means of comfort and soul-rest.* Reflect a moment on the nature of this present life, with all its cares, bitter disappointments, sad bereavements, anxieties for those we love, and its burdens of disease, poverty and age, and consider how direful man's condition without the sweet solace of prayer. In such a world as this who can estimate the value of such promises as these: "In nothing be anxious; but in everything by prayer and supplication with thanksgiving let your requests

be made known unto God. And the peace of God which pas-
seth all understanding, shall guard your hearts and your
thoughts in Christ Jesus." (Phil. 4:6, 7) "Casting all your anxiety upon him, because he careth for you." (I Pet. 5:7) A heart
that is cold and callous, and insensible to the sorrows and
woes of the world, and to its own perils, may not feel the need
of prayer; but a heart, tender and responsive to others' woes,
and realizing the awful peril of sin, and with a sympathy so
deep and wide that like the Master it can weep over the sins
and sorrows of others, would break but for the solace and
strength found in prayer. Who of us that have known much
of life's bitter experiences, have not felt, at times, that if we
could not go into the solitude of our own chamber, and there,
alone with God, pour out our soul to him, and seek his divine
sympathy and strength, we would break down under the
heavy burden? And who of us, in such an hour, when all the
world has seemed dark to us, has ever gone to him in vain?
Has not our experience enabled us to sing,

> *"O how praying rests the weary!*
> *Prayer will change the night to day;*
> *So, when life seems dark and dreary,*
> *Don't forget to pray."*

What profit in prayer? Ask the toil-worn pilgrim, who,
staff in hand, is nearing the gates of the golden city, and
whose hoary head reflects the light of the eternal day, and he
will tell you that without it he could not have climbed the difficult paths of self-denial and patient endurance by which he
has reached the precincts of the heavenly city. Ask the bat-
tle-scarred hero of the cross, who, after many conflicts, is
about laying down life's burden to take up the crown, and he
will tell you that by prayer he gained the victory in every

contest. Ask that aged mother in Israel, on whose brow there sets the jewel of heavenly peace, and on whose sweet face there shines the light,

"That never shone on land or sea,"

how she has brought out of all her life-struggles and sorrows, the serenity of spirit and the triumphant faith which awaits with fond expectation the reunion of loved ones gone before on that "far-off shore," and she will tell you that prayer has sweetened all the bitter waters of life for her, and lightened all her burdens.

Ask the great spirits—the heroic men and women—who are now at the front, in the thick of life's battles, bearing the sneers and reproaches of the world as the representatives of the great social, political and religious reforms of our time, whence they derive strength and courage to oppose popular evils, and endure poverty and scorn for their advocacy of right and truth, and they will tell you that their power comes from above, and is received through prayer.

And let me say to the young people who may read these pages, if any of you entertain the idea, that you can very greatly influence this world for good by any brilliancy of genius, wealth of talent, or capacity for work, which you may possess, aside from the aid which you can only receive through prayer, you have greatly over-estimated your own strength, and under-estimated the magnitude of the difficulties in the way. "Our sufficiency is of God," and it is only as we link hands with him, and are upheld by him that we can make our lives a great potency for good in the world. Learn this, young friends, and if you are proposing to yourselves great life-tasks, which will enroll your names among earth's benefactors, or to lift your characters in any wise above the common mass, make up your minds to spend much of your time in company with God, seeking his counsel, becoming imbued with his Spirit, and being conformed to his image. Prayer is the golden key which unlocks the treasure-vaults of heaven.

Truly, as England's Poet Laureate has said:

> *More things are wrought by prayer*
> *Than this world dreams of. Wherefore let thy voice*
> *Rise like a fountain for me night and day.*
> *For what are men better than sheep or goats*
> *That nourish a blind life within the brain,*
> *If, knowing God, they lift not hands of prayer*
> *Both for themselves and those who call them friend?*
> *For so the whole round earth is every way*
> *Bound by gold chains about the feet of God.*

Prayer

O God of all consolation and comfort, whose delight it is, out of your infinite fullness to satisfy the wants of all your creatures, and to grant peace and strength to the troubled hearts of all your children, we thank you that you have ordained prayer as the method of our soul's access to you, and by which we may find the rest and peace which we so much need. It is with gratitude and thankfulness that I recall the times when you have heard the voice of my supplication and have lightened my burden and have given new strength to my fainting heart. Surely, O Lord, you have shown yourself to be a present help in time of trouble. When in sickness, you have raised me up; when in doubt and perplexity, you have guided my steps; when in sorrow and mental distress, you have breathed upon my soul your infinite peace; when in sickness and fear I have called upon your name, you have given me health and courage. So that I may exclaim with the Psalmist, "Blessed be the Lord, because he hath heard the voice of my supplications. My heart hath trusted in him and I am helped. Therefore my heart greatly rejoices; and with my song will I praise him." O help me, heavenly Father, more and more to realize the blessedness of prayer, and learn to come boldly unto a throne of grace that I may obtain mercy and find grace to help in time of need. In all the trials, temptations and sorrows that may await me, may I always resort to you as my surest defense, my consolation and abiding Friend, and my soul's chief delight. And this I ask in the name of Christ. Amen!

10. Hindrances to Prayer

Ye ask and receive not, because ye ask amiss.

JAMES 4: 3

So many and so great are the benefits of prayer, that no one who appreciates them can fail to be interested in the question as to what are some of the chief hindrances to its exercise. It is a common experience with most of us, that when we have tried to pray, there has been the absence of that joy, comfort and peace which true prayer always brings to the soul. For this there must be some cause, and the reason will always be found in us, not in God, who is always gracious, and whose ears are ever open to the cry of the righteous. It is my purpose now to seek for some of these causes that hinder prayer, and make it unavailing.

1.   The first of these is *impenitence*. The impenitent man never prays. When it was said of Saul of Tarsus, "Behold he prayeth!" there was furnished the highest possible proof that he was penitent for his past sins, and was a changed man, no longer to be dreaded and shunned as a persecutor of Christ. This is because prayer implies certain conditions that cannot co-exist with impenitence, such as faith in God, a proper reverence for his name, consciousness of our spiritual needs,

and a hungering and thirsting after righteousness. The impenitent man has no taste for prayer. The desire to pray is about the first sign of true penitence. He that has no relish for prayer, when *alone with God*, and feels no impulse to lift his soul up to God, in confession, adoration, thanksgiving and petition, may well be alarmed at his spiritual state. How dare such a one call himself a disciple of the praying Christ?

Sometimes the soul is driven to prayer by a sense of duty or obligation, or, it may be, of *habit*, and experiences no spontaneity of emotion, no joy, no strength of desire, no consciousness of personal communion with God. The words we utter, in a mechanical way, express desires that our souls do not feel, and they seem to rise no higher than our heads. This experience is not infrequently described as God withdrawing his face from us, but a moment's reflection must convince us that the *real* cause of this state of things is to be found in us, not in God. "Behold, the Lord's hand is not shortened, that it cannot save; neither his ear heavy, that it cannot hear: but your iniquities have separated between you and your God, and your sins have hid his face from you, that he will not hear. For your hands are defiled with blood, and your fingers with iniquity; your lips have spoken lies, your tongue muttereth wickedness." (Isaiah 59:1-3)

Nor is it true to suppose that nothing but gross immorality could thus hinder our prayers. The soul, like the eye, is delicately organized, and a very subtle form of sin may suffice to quench the spirit of prayer. "It does not require," says a recent writer of national renown, "what the world would call a great sin, to break up the serenity of the soul in its devotional hours. The experience of prayer has delicate complications. A little thing, secreted there, may dislocate its mechanism and arrest its movement…. Even a doubtful principle of life, harbored in the heart, is perilous to the peacefulness of devotion. May not many of us find the cause of our joylessness in prayer, in the fact that we are living upon some unsettled principle of conduct? I apprehend that there is very much of suspense of conscience among Christians, upon subjects of practical life on which there is no suspense of action" (Austin Phelps, *The Still Hour*).

2. *Wrong motives in prayer*, often vitiate them. An instance of this is given in the text quoted at the head of this chapter. "Ye ask and receive not, because ye ask amiss, that ye may spend it in your pleasures." One may ask God for wealth, that he may excel his neighbors in luxurious living and gratify a whole brood of fleshly desires. Another may ask for health or position, that he may use these things for his own pleasure. It is possible, even, to desire spiritual power and unction, the gift of tongues in prayer and preaching, in order that we may thereby gain conspicuity and the honors of the world, along with our increased usefulness. Alas! How deceitful is the human heart! And how seldom do we stop to analyze our motives in asking God for what we desire! Not seldom would we feel abashed at our temerity did we always face squarely the real motives that prompt many of our petitions.

3. *Insincerity*. This may seem to be a grave charge to bring against the prayers of Christians, but we venture to mention it among the actual causes that prevent many of our prayers from being answered. What I mean by it is that we often ask for things that we do not really desire. Our judgment is convinced that the things we ask for are things we ought to desire, and that Christians ought to pray for, and so we utter with our lips petitions which our hearts do not endorse. When we pray for the spirit of self-denial, for instance, do we always really desire that this spirit shall so

possess us that we may be willing to give up all for Christ's sake? When we ask that all obstacles to Christian growth and usefulness be taken out of our way, do we mean all that this may involve? Suppose it means poverty, trials and sore chastening, are we ready to endure these things for the sake of obtaining higher spiritual good? Here again I cannot forbear quoting from Austin Phelps, in *The Still Hour*, that prince of devotional writers, of whose classic pages I have availed myself elsewhere.

"Many of the prime objects of prayer enchant us only in the distance, Brought near to us, and in concrete forms, and made to grow lifelike in our conceptions, they very sensibly abate the pulse of our desire to possess them, because we cannot but discover that, to realize them in our lives, certain other darling objects must be sacrificed which we are not yet willing to part with. The paradox is true to the life, that a man may even *fear* an answer to his prayers….

He has not really desired that God would give heed to him, for any other purpose than to give him an hour of pleasurable devotional excitement. That his objects of prayer should actually be inwrought into his character, and should live in his own consciousness, is by no means the thing he has been thinking of, and is the last thing he is ready just now to wish for."

4. *False views of prayer*. In another chapter, I have given some attention to that theory of prayer that makes it wholly subjective in its effect. It is easy to see how such a theory, once fully accepted, would undermine faith in the value of prayer, and gradually lead to its neglect. That which gives an inexpressible charm, and infinite value to prayer is the plain, scriptural idea, that it is a child of God talking, out of his heart, to his loving heavenly Father, who inclines his ear and

listens to his earthborn child with a deep and tender concern. Hold on to that simple faith, dear reader, if you would value rightly the "sweet hour of prayer," whether it be alone with God, or in the assembly of his saints.

Another mistaken view of prayer is, that if God does not answer us *in the way* which we expect and desire, and *at the time* when we think he ought to answer, that he does not hear us at all and our prayer is vain. Hence we cease to pray. This is a mistaken view of prayer. God has not placed in our hands so dangerous a weapon as prayer would be if it at once secured *what* we asked and *in the way* and *at the time* we desire. This would be to abdicate his throne in favor of man, and allow us to exercise unlimited power to our own destruction. God is too good and too wise to do that. He knows what is best for us, and his goodness and mercy are as manifest in withholding many of the things we ask for, as in granting others.

> *"We, ignorant of ourselves,*
>   *Beg often our own harms, which the wise powers*
> *Deny us for our good; so find we profit,*
>   *By losing our prayers."*   SHAKESPEARE

It was this erroneous view of prayer that led some people to doubt the efficacy of prayer, because the life of President Garfield was not spared in answer to the prayers of the nation. More than once it has happened, in my own experience, that God has answered my prayers in a way *directly opposite* from that which I expected and hoped for. At the *time* the answers were not recognized, as such, but in the light of subsequent events it became clear to me that God had heard my prayer and had answered me in his own way, which of course was far better than my way. That this is equally true in many instances where we cannot so clearly recognize it, does not admit of doubt. "For my thoughts are not your thoughts, neither are your ways my ways, saith the Lord. For as the heavens are higher than the earth, so are my ways higher than your ways and my thoughts than your thoughts." (Isaiah 55:8, 9)

5. *Environment*. By this convenient word, I mean that the surroundings and associations of Christians, growing out of their business or social companionships, are often unfavorable to the devotional spirit and to the habit of prayer. A man whose business throws him into association with men whose controlling motives are avarice, ambition and worldly pride, must be an unusually devout man not to be injuriously affected thereby. If we add to this what is not infrequently true, that the business itself, in its methods at least, is of doubtful moral propriety, we have a combination of circumstances in which the spirit of devotion cannot thrive. It is certain to be frozen out. In such cases, a man has to choose between his business and his soul. He cannot serve God and Mammon, and must make his choice between them.

Young Christians often find that their social comradeship is of such a character as to disincline them to personal piety and to devotional habits. They lose their relish for the lone hour with God, or for the house of God, just in proportion as they drink into the spirit of their companions. As soon as this is discovered, there ought to be no hesitation as to the safe course to pursue. Let there be a change of associates. If this is not possible, see that there is a change in the character of the amusements and entertainments indulged in. Why should not Christian young people become a positive, molding force in society, so reconstructing its social life as to make it intellectually and morally helpful? If Christians are "the light of the world," they should let their light *shine*, and not hide it under a bushel.

6. *Lack of proper mental and spiritual food.* Not more is a sound and healthful body dependent on well prepared, nutritious food, than is the mind and heart on suitable mental and spiritual nutriment. Much of the reading done by the young people of today is a positive hindrance to spiritual and mental growth, and the devotional spirit withers and dies under its influence. I feel that I should be recreant to my duty to the young people of this generation, not to warn them against that species of literature which creates a disrelish for sober reading, especially for the Scriptures, and is fatal to the devotional spirit. I make no indiscriminate war against fiction, much of which is healthful and helpful, but there can be no doubt that the habit of indiscriminate reading of light and fictitious literature has sapped the spiritual life and vigor of many Christians, both young and old.

In the cities it is not uncommon that the daily papers, with their record of crimes of all sorts and their sensational news and social gossip, furnish the staple mental food for many older people, even members of evangelical churches. Is it any wonder that this class of people have no time for family worship, and for private devotions, and no relish for either? How could it be otherwise? They do not read the Bible with any regularity, and often read no religious papers or books. Their spiritual nature dies of starvation, or of poisonous food. Set this down as true: *The daily, reverent reading of God's word is essential to the maintenance of devotional habits.* It alone is capable of creating the atmosphere in which the spirit of true piety is fostered and sustained. Hence, it will be found universal, we think, that the neglect of prayer is evermore accompanied with the neglect of Bible reading and study.

7. *Lack of meditation and self-examination.* Though I have adverted to this subject elsewhere, I mention it here among

the causes that hinder prayer, or make it formal and joyless. Prayer, to be acceptable to God, must be related to the soul's needs. It must be the sincere expression of the soul's inmost desires. But unless we pause awhile, in the quiet of our own chamber, and introspect our hearts and lives, and examine ourselves in the light of God's word, there can be no intelligent appreciation of our needs and no fervency of desire for those spiritual blessings which alone can satisfy the soul. My own experience and observation lead me to believe that, ordinarily, prayer lacks both in fervor and definiteness when it is not preceded by a few moments of thoughtful meditation in connection with the reading of the Scriptures. I am also convinced that one of the great evils of our modern life, is that we have allowed business, social pleasures, and other things to rob us of the quiet hour when we can be alone with God in private devotion. Without this solitude, and the quiet meditation for which it gives opportunity, there are apt to be wanting two important elements of successful prayer, namely: *definiteness in our petitions, and intensity of desire.*

Prayer

O you who hear prayer, help us to pray aright. We know not what we should pray for as we ought, but we rejoice that the Holy Spirit helps our infirmities and interprets our inarticulate groanings before the throne of God. Graciously aid us, O God, in putting away from our thoughts and our lives all those things that hinder prayer and prevent our Christian growth and usefulness. Help us to come before you with clean hands and with pure hearts, and to seek those blessings that will enrich our spiritual life and adorn our characters. O search us, and if there be any evil way in us, any unworthy motive, any secret sin, any unholy desire, which renders our prayers unacceptable to you, enable us to purge ourselves from all such faults, that our communion with you may be sweet and profitable to us. Remove our transgressions far from us, O Lord, and restore unto us the joys of your salvation. So shall we call upon your name with gladness and you shall answer us in showers of descending mercy. And this we ask in Christ's name. Amen!

11. Prayer as a Habit of the Soul

⬥

Pray without ceasing.   I THES. 5:13

As it is not possible to be always in an attitude of formal prayer, some have found difficulty with the above passage, while the experience of others has interpreted to them the apostle's meaning. One important aspect of prayer is communion with God, and this state or condition of the soul is the normal one for a Christian. The passage above cited means, no doubt, that this attitude should become the fixed habit of the soul. Prayer, in this sense, is not to be regarded simply as a distinct religious exercise having its own set time, but as a process woven into the very texture of the Christian's mind, and covering the whole domain of life in all its length and breadth. "Like the golden thread in a tissue," to use another's simile, "it frequently disappears beneath the common threads, and is hidden from the eye; yet nevertheless it is substantially there. Like a stream running underground for a certain period of its course, and then reappearing," so underneath the surface of our every day life, there may run a continuous stream of prayer.

One does not have to live a Christian life very long in the midst of life's labors, temptations and conflicts, until he learns that the stated, formal prayers, morning and evening, though indispensable, are by no means adequate for the needs of the heart, and he will soon find himself sending upwards, all through the busy day, brief, unspoken petitions or thanksgivings, whispered only in the secret chamber of the soul but heard in heaven. What a relief this is to the Christian bearing special burdens of sorrow, of temptation or of anxiety, every faithful disciple can testify. This is what is called ejaculatory prayer. It waits on no times or seasons. It calls for no cessation of the busy labor of the day. It depends not on solitude or silence. It leaps from the heart as we travel along the crowded mart, or sit conversing with friends, or pause a moment before some perplexing question on which we need light from above.

It would be a great mistake to confine prayer to particular times and places, instead of allowing it to spread over all the day and all our conscious hours, and to rise up in a spontaneous stream towards heaven whenever the opportunity or the need of it is suggested. These ejaculatory prayers, however, are not to take the place of our stated times of prayer. Rather, they prepare us for such seasons of prayer and make them far more enjoyable. The heart that goes from morning until evening without once lifting itself up in the interstices of business, toward God, in a silent petition or an inarticulate word of thanks, will not come to the evening worship with that keen spiritual relish which the soul experiences that often during the day has found time to think of God and offer its loving homage to him.

When the heart is beset with anxieties, and burdened with care, it cannot well wait for relief until the regular hour for prayer arrives, but goes at once to God for his strength and guidance. To all such hearts, the habit of ejaculatory prayer is a blessing of inestimable value. By means of it, they are enabled, right in the stress of the emergency, to enter into the closet of their own heart, shut the door, and speak into the ear of a sympathetic and Infinite Father. Here they find refuge in the midst of the storm, and a haven in which they may anchor and find rest and peace. The case of Nehemiah, in the presence of Artaxerxes the king, when asked to state what he wished, is an instance of the value of this kind of prayer. In a moment of supreme interest to the affairs of his people, he carries his cause to God and then boldly requests that he be permitted to return to Jerusalem to rebuild the temple and city, which is readily granted. (Nehemiah 2:1-9) How brief this prayer must have been, and yet how all potent in its results! Blessed is the man who has such a command over his mind, and such a *habit* of prayer, that in these sudden emergencies of life he can instantly withdraw into the recesses of his own heart and send upward a prayer to God. Those who travel in foreign lands, far from loved ones, esteem it a great privilege, and a great achievement of modern science, that they can communicate in a few moments, by means of the submarine cable and telegraph system, with the dear ones at home. And so it is. But how much greater the privilege, and more marvelous the fact, that we can on any part of the earth, in mid-ocean or in the wilds of an African forest, in a moment send a message to God and receive his response! But can we always know that God hears us? Yes, if we ask according to God's will, for "this is the boldness which we have toward him, that if we ask anything according to his will he heareth us; and if we know that he heareth us whatsoever we ask, we know that we have the petitions which we have asked of him." (John 5:14,15) Whether the petition be for yourself, or for one near and dear to you, know that it has been heard, and if in accordance with God's will, has been granted.

Happily, the value of prayer does not depend on the number of words we employ, but upon the degree of earnestness and faith with which it is presented. "Lord, save, or I perish!" was quite sufficient to bring the Master to Peter's side, on that stormy night on Galilee. Could we always pray thus, we would have less occasion to mourn over unanswered prayers. But let us not think of brief, ejaculatory prayer as appropriate only to sudden emergencies, or times of sore trial. To what Christian, given to prayer and communion with God, does there not come, often during the busiest days, a sweet remembrance of God's loving kindness, and merciful providence? How delightful it is, at such times, to lift the heart to God in a moment of thanksgiving and adoration. And this habit tends to bring to our remembrance the unnumbered benefits which we receive from the hand of God, and which we are too prone to forget. Thankfulness for mercies received is the best preparation of heart for seeking additional favors. The impulse to offer thanksgiving to God, or to present a petition to him, comes from the Spirit of God, and should not be resisted, no matter what our surroundings may be at the time, as it need not interfere with the demands of business or of social intercourse.

These reflections, it is hoped, will help us to understand better what the apostle means by his exhortation to "pray without ceasing." Prayer, it is seen, is not a thing to be shut up in one corner of the day, or limited to a brief space in the morning and evening; but it is a pervading habit of the soul which is to shed its holy and hallowing influence over all the hours, and to maintain unbroken communion with God. Such a habit once formed, it would be comparatively easy to adopt that other law of life laid down by the same apostle; that "whatsoever ye do, in word or in deed, do all in the name of the Lord Jesus, giving thanks to God the Father through him." (Col. 3:17). This passage is especially significant in connecting our religious life with our other everyday duties, and mingling prayer with those deeds that are related directly to the material side of our nature. This shows that Christianity is not a religion for the closet, only, but that it is intended to sanctify all the relations and duties of this present life.

Prayer

Almighty God, who has manifested yourself unto us as Father, Son and Holy Spirit, grant unto me, I beseech you, the spirit of prayer and of supplication. May there be such strong affinity between my soul and you, that prayer shall become a most delightful habit of my life, and I may be able to say with your servant of old, "I will trust in the Lord at all times; His praise shall continually be in my mouth." Will you give me such a sense of your gracious care, O God, and of your amazing mercy to me in Jesus Christ, that my heart may overflow with thankfulness to you, often, in the busy hours of the day; and if any great trial or sorrow come upon me, help me instinctively to fly to you for refuge, as the bird flies to its mountain with the coming of the storm, or the darkness. For the blessed privilege of instant and constant access to you in prayer, I do most sincerely thank you, and beseech you to help me wisely and reverently to avail myself of it in every time of need, and at every impulse of your spirit. Hear my prayer for Christ's sake. Amen!

12. Watchfulness

Keep thy heart with all diligence; For out of it are the issues of life.
PROV. 4: 23

"What, could ye not watch with me one hour? Watch and pray that ye enter not into temptation; the spirit indeed is willing, but the flesh is weak.
MATT. 26: 40

The command to "watch" may be said to be one of the key words of Christ to his disciples. The duty of prayer is not more clearly emphasized in the New Testament than that of watchfulness. The command means *wakefulness* and *alertness*, as against moral drowsiness and indifference. It implies that we are in the enemy's country, in the midst of foes, and need to be constantly on guard. The command to *watch*, so often urged on Christians, may be regarded as including at least the following duties:

1. *Self-examination.* Perhaps there is no precaution for spiritual safety more frequently neglected, and with more disastrous results, than the faithful examination of one's inmost thoughts, purposes and motives—the inner tendencies of one's life. The precept of Solomon, to "keep thy heart with all diligence, for out of it are the issues of life," is emphasized by Christ, who taught the Pharisees that it is

not anything without the man that defiles him, but that which proceeds out of him. "For from within, out of the heart of men, evil thoughts proceed—fornications, thefts, murders, adulteries, covetings, wickednesses, deceit, lasciviousness, an evil eye, railing, pride, foolishness: all these evil things proceed from within and defile the man" (Mark 7:21-23). What a fearful brood of unclean things is this, to be hatched in the human heart! No wonder we are admonished to guard it with all diligence, and that Christ should say, "Blessed are the pure in heart." The first duty of a Christian, then, would seem to be to watch his thoughts and desires, the very fountain of one's life whence flow the deeds and the words that are pure or impure according as the heart is.

There is frequently a moral cowardice which prevents one from fearlessly examining into the real condition of his inner life, not unlike that which keeps some businessmen from a searching examination of their books, lest they be found bankrupt, or certain morbid invalids from having a too critical diagnosis of their physical condition, lest it be found incurable. It is plain that all this is unwise, because it is an unsafe course. An honest man should know the exact condition of his business; a diseased man, if he be wise, will seek to understand the real nature of his malady, that he may be healed, if possible, and if not, then to arrange his affairs accordingly. Why should it be different with our moral disorders? Are not the motives still infinitely higher for an honest introspection of our hearts to know their real condition?

A thoughtful writer on this subject presents a mighty motive for diligence in keeping the heart, as the only way of successfully resisting temptation. He says: "It will be found that all the more grievous faults of the tempted soul come from this—that the keeping of the heart has been neglected, that the evil has not been nipped in the bud. We have allowed matters to advance to a question of conduct—'Shall I say this, or not say it? Do this or not do it?' Whereas the stand should have been made higher up, and the ground disputed in the inner man. As if the mere restraint upon outward conduct, without the homage of the heart to God's law, could avail us aught, or be anything else than an offensive hypocrisy in the eyes of the Heart-searcher! As if Balaam's refraining from the malediction of the lips, while his heart was going after his covetousness, could be acceptable to the Almighty!….There is therefore no safety for us except in making our stand at the avenues of the will, and rejecting at once every questionable impulse. And this, it is obvious, cannot be done without watchfulness and self-recollection—without a continual bearing in mind where, and what we are, and that we have a treasure in our keeping of which our foes seek to rob us. Endeavor to make your heart a little sanctuary, in which you may continually realize the Presence of God, and from which unhallowed thoughts, and even vain thoughts, must be carefully excluded."

But young Christians may as well know at once, what older ones have found out by experience, that the only way to guard the heart against evil thoughts is to admit Christ into it, and enthrone him there. Once your affections are centered on him, and he is made the ruler of your life and conduct, all that is unholy and impure will flee from his presence. As he cleansed the temple, by driving out the thieves, the covetous and the extortioners from its sacred precincts, so will he, if once admitted, banish from the temple of our heart, the whole nest of evil thoughts which hatch into crimes of various kinds, if they are harbored there. That is the reason he knocks at the door of our hearts for admittance; he wishes to purify them and dwell there.

The lesson of self-distrust, or our own inability to keep our heart pure without the divine power dwelling within us, is one of the hardest for us to learn. Sometimes it requires several humiliating falls to teach us how incapable we are of coping with our great adversary, and to bring us to commit our souls to "him who is able to keep us from falling and to present us faultless before the presence of his glory with exceeding joy." But if we watch carefully the inner tendencies of the heart, we cannot fail to discover the need of a higher power than our own in order to guard all its approaches against the assaults of evil. It is for this reason that prayer is associated with watchfulness in Christ's teaching. Prayer is the expression of our dependence upon God, human weakness throwing itself upon divine strength, and human ignorance leaning upon divine wisdom. "Watch and pray, lest ye enter into temptation." Neither without the other is a sufficient protection against the wiles of the devil.

When such personal introspection as is here recommended has discovered the weak point in one's character, special and almost exclusive attention should be given first to fortifying such point until it has been made strong. In character building, as in almost every other great undertaking, singleness of aim is the surest road to success. Attack your besetting sin, whatever that may be, with all the concentrated energy of thought, prayer and effort. "The 'one thing needful,'" says a discriminating writer on this subject, "for those beset with any moral and spiritual infirmity, is to rid themselves of it, rooting it, as far as possible, out of their hearts, with loathing and abhorrence. Until this is achieved there is no business to them of equal importance."

2. *Alertness, or readiness for action*, is another element of watchfulness. The first point might have been called "The

Inlook," and the second, "The Outlook." It would be a great mistake to suppose that all our time for self-improvement should be devoted to looking in on our own thoughts, motives and purposes. This would produce a morbid spiritual condition that would prove an obstacle alike to happiness and to spiritual growth.

What is needed is to know our own spiritual state, and when introspection has accomplished this, the eye of the soul should look out and, above all, should look up. Some of the things to look out for are,

a.   The movements of the enemy, the devices of Satan for entrapping the souls of the unwary. Those practices, forms of amusement, places of resort, habits and associations that lure many to destruction, avoid. Why should you incur risks that have proved fatal in so many instances? "Lead me not into temptation," is a most wise prayer, but if we walk into these temptations, our prayer is a mockery.

b.   Opportunities for doing good. Unless we are on the alert, we will allow many golden opportunities to pass by unimproved. The kind word we might have spoken to cheer a discouraged heart, the gentle reproof, which might have saved a soul front sin, the loving deed done in Christ's name to the poor and needy, all these were neglected because we were not watching for opportunities to do good.

> *"O the world is full of sighs,*
> *Full of sad and weeping eyes;*
> *Help your fallen brother rise,*
> *While the days are going by."*

c.   The signs of the times. Christ reproved his disciples for their inattention to the signs of the great times in which they lived. The most stupendous events were occurring before their eyes, prophecy was being fulfilled, a new era was being brought to birth, but they seemed not to comprehend the meaning of these things. Had they done so, how much better they might have performed their part in the great drama that was being enacted! But may we not live in a time full of momentous issues, "in an age on ages telling?" Let us seek to know the times in which we live and the great crises of history. We are commanded to watch for the Coming of the Son of Man, the great event of the future, and to be ready, lest he find us slumbering, or with lamps untrimmed or unsupplied with oil. The best state of readiness for the coming of Christ, is a condition of eagerness to know and readiness to do his will.

So watching and praying and toiling, we shall see Christ growing in our own characters, and the world's long night of sin and sorrow growing gray with the streaks of the coming light, and all the eastern hilltops glow with the radiance of his coming, whose advent shall usher in the eternal day.

Prayer

O you All-seeing God, whose eye penetrates into all the secret places of our hearts and minds, help me to see myself, in some measure, as your see me, and to know my own weaknesses and faults, to the end that I may be able to overcome them through your gracious aid. In view of the dangers and temptations that surround me, help me to be ever watchful, examining myself, in my secret thoughts and purposes, and to be wary of Satan's devices. Grant me grace and courage, O Lord, to resist the very beginnings of evil, in the heart, and to refuse to entertain thoughts or desires that are contrary to your will. Enable me to be ready for every good word and work, and to seek out opportunities of being useful. Give me a tender regard for the welfare of all your children and a deep concern for the salvation of all men. Help me, O you blessed Savior, to watch with you, until the time of temptation is past. Let the words of my mouth and the meditation of my heart, be acceptable, in your sight, O Lord, my Strength and my Redeemer. Amen!

13. The Mission of Suffering

And not only so, but let us also rejoice in our tribulations; knowing that tribulation worketh patience; and patience probation, and probation hope.

ROMANS 5: 3, 4

For it became him for whom are all things, and through whom are all things, in bringing many sons unto glory, to make the author of their salvation perfect through sufferings.

HEB. 2:10

The apostle having just exhorted his brethren to "rejoice in the hope of the glory of God," thinks of the present trials and sufferings which surround us here, and, as if feeling the soul's need of consolation in things nearer at hand, immediately adds: "And not only so, but let us also rejoice in our tribulations." Certainly if there is any philosophy of life, or any attainment of faith, that will enable the Christian to extract joy out of the very trials and calamities of life, it is greatly worth our while to seek it as a most invaluable possession. Many Christian lives are comparatively joyless, because of life's crosses, disappointments and bereavements. Many of us have not yet attained to that sublime height of faith that will enable us to say with Paul, "Let us also rejoice in tribulations;" or with James, "Count it all joy, my brethren, when ye fall into manifold temptations." (James 1:2). And yet these men of God, speaking out of their experience, no doubt, as well as by divine guidance, were able to give substantial reasons for rejoicing in trials and tribulations. Let us examine some of the reasons that justify us, as they did these ancient servants of Jesus Christ, in regarding these tribulations, not as hindrances, but as helps in the development of Christian character.

1. *Tribulation works patience.* Paul and James both assign this fact as a reason for rejoicing in tribulation. James says, "Knowing that *the proof of your faith* worketh patience," regarding these trials which come upon us here as so many proofs or tests of our faith. It is stated, not as a theory, but as a fact, that trials or tribulations work patience. Christian experience, in all the centuries that have come and gone since then, but corroborates the truth of the statement. It were scarcely worth our while, now and here, to stop for the purpose of inquiring into, the philosophy of this fact, seeing that all experience attests its reality. Rather let us inquire if patience be a virtue of sufficient value to reward us for enduring tribulation. In its current use, the word patience signifies little more than passive resistance to evil, the calm endurance of suffering. Even this is great gain; but the original, besides this passive element, implies "an active perseverance, a brave persistence in good works, that will not be shaken by fear of evil, and an abiding hope of final victory which no present dangers may disturb." It is a heroic virtue, that, having counted the cost, endures to the end. Job was noted for his patience, but its highest exemplification, of course, is to be seen in Jesus. No fretfulness, impatience or worry marred the beauty or dissipated the energies of that perfect life. How we admire it in him! But how much more does he admire it in his followers!

If trials, misfortunes, disappointments, persecution for truth's sake, or sickness, do but serve to make me more patient, more like my Master, why should not I take some joy in them?

2. *Patience works probation*, or approval. Rotherham renders the word—*a-putting-to-the-test*. *Approval* seems to be supported by the best authority—being the *result* of "probation" or of "putting-to-the-test," which the context seems to require. Or, if we blend the two renderings and read, "patience worketh probation resulting in approval," we will not miss the thought very far. It is clear that without patience to endure tribulation, the soul would be deprived of a necessary discipline, for it is only to those in whom patience is permitted to do its perfect work, that tribulation yields its beneficent results. But when patience fortifies the soul to endure, meekly, all the adversities of life—its losses, its pains, its sorrows, its temptations and conflicts—it inevitably results in approval, the approval of one's own conscience, and God's approval. Who can estimate the value of such approval? Its influence must stimulate the whole spiritual nature and impart new vigor to the religious life. One of its most marked results is the implantation or intensification of hope.

3. Hence, *probation (or approval) works hope*. What an inspiring factor in Christian life hope is, every true disciple of Jesus knows. It is mentioned by Paul along with faith and love, as one of the things that abide. To the Roman brethren who were suffering great affliction he says, "We are saved by hope." It alone could have strengthened the heart and nerved the arm of the early Christians for the conflicts of those perilous days. Now, as then, it is "as an anchor of the soul, a hope both sure and steadfast, and entering into that which is within the veil." Hope ever sings of a brighter tomorrow. In the midst of poverty, disease, privation, toil and conflict, it looks

away to that fair land where there is no more sickness, hunger, sorrow, crying or death, and cheerfully bears the present, temporary ill, in expectation of future everlasting good. Such is hope, the child of probation, which is the child of tribulation. "Thus through a series of virtues, each in turn effect and cause, tribulation is 'the nurse of our hope in the world to come.'"

It is very difficult, while we are in the midst of these manifold trials, to take this cheerful and scriptural view of their meaning and purpose. We find ourselves inclined to doubt whether the particular trial or tribulation to which we are at the time subjected, belongs to the class which work out beneficial results, until we remember that this same apostle declares, in another place, that, "to them that love God all things work together for good, even to them that are called according to his purpose." (Rom. 8:29) It cannot be doubted, then, that our particular and peculiar trial belongs to the "all things" that "work together for good." How manifold and various are the tribulations which assail us here! There is loss of property and of friends, there is poverty, unrequited toil, disappointed hopes, frustrated plans, false friends, ungrateful and wayward children, wasting disease destroying the life of loved ones, misrepresentation and persecution, and evermore the temptations of Satan. To all these are to be added the routine of daily duties, which are sometimes irksome and onerous. What a splendid philosophy is that which Christian faith lays hold of, by which all these seeming calamities and adversities are transformed into so many kind providential agencies designed to promote our spiritual growth and development!

We are inclined to forget the divine mission of suffering. Even Jesus, the sinless One, "was made perfect through suffering." There were qualifications and elements of character essential to his high office as the world's Savior, which could only be gained by personal experience with human sorrow and suffering. Hence he was "a man of sorrows and acquainted with grief." His life was one of almost constant contact with disease, misfortune, poverty, and sin. He bore our sorrows and suffered for our iniquities. Out of it all there came a character, not only sinless, but how full of tenderness, compassion and sympathy. It is the mission of suffering not only to test faith, produce patience, work out probation and intensify hope, but also to mellow the heart, widen our sympathies, burn out the dross in our nature and purify the gold, and qualify us for helpful ministries to all other suffering ones of earth. Why then should we expect to be wafted to heaven

> *"on flowery beds of ease,*
> *While others fought to win the prize*
> *And sailed through bloody seas?"*

To learn this lesson—that all life's crosses and trials and conflicts, and the performance of our daily tasks, no matter how humble, are the very means which God has ordained for our spiritual discipline, and the stepping-stones by which we are to rise from earth to heaven, from bitter sorrows and lowly duties to celestial joys and heavenly employments—is to know the meaning of life and to master the secret of contentment and happiness in our earthly lot. Having learned this lesson we may "rejoice in tribulation," for we can see, then, how it is, that "our light affliction, which is for the moment, worketh for us more and more exceedingly, an eternal weight of glory," (II Cor. 4:17) and. we may, with the same apostle, "reckon that the sufferings of this present time are not worthy to be compared with the glory which shall be revealed to us-ward." (Rom. 8:18)

These comforting thoughts, I would commend to the afflicted, the burdened, the persecuted, and the tempted and tried ones. Rest assured that your loving Father in heaven knows your special trial, means it for your eternal good, and will not allow you to be tempted above that you are able to bear in his name and strength. Let us not forget the exhortation of which Paul reminded his Hebrew brethren who were suffering great tribulation:

> *"My son, regard not lightly the chastening of the Lord,*
> *Nor faint, when thou art reproved of him;*
> *For whom the Lord loveth, he chasteneth,*
> *And scourgeth every son whom he receiveth."*
>
> *HEB. 12:5,6*

It is true, as the apostle adds, that "All chastening seemeth for the present to be, not joyous, but grievous," yet it is also true, nevertheless, that "afterward it yieldeth peaceable fruit unto them that have been exercised thereby, even the fruit of righteousness." It is the "afterward" that God has in view, for the spiritual results of chastening are eternal, while the tribulations are only for a short time.

As the voyager across the ocean soon forgets the storms and the billows which filled his soul with fears, and made his passage uncomfortable, when he has reached his destination and is welcomed by kind friends, so we, tempest-tossed passengers on life's stormy sea, when safely anchored in the quiet haven of everlasting peace, shall find our past sorrows and afflictions swallowed up in the supreme delight of the beatific vision. There, on some fair mount of vision, looking back over our earthly struggles, and trials, we shall see clearly, as we cannot here and now, that God's way with us was ordered in mercy, and that life's shadows, no less than its sunshine, are proofs of his amazing love. Meanwhile, "we walk by faith, not by sight."

But if, while walking by faith, we have been enabled to rejoice in the tribulations of this life, because of the spiritual education which they bring, what must be the joy and delight of the triumphant soul, when we shall walk by sight amid the glories and splendors of the unseen world! What a vision of immortal beauty awaits the transition of God's children from the body, with its pains and temptations, into the paradise of God! What radiant forms of celestial dignity shall pass before us! We shall see the King in his beauty, and look with unveiled faces upon the divine glory. Scenes, of which earth's fairest landscapes are but faint suggestions, will burst upon the view of earth's weary pilgrims, who, having walked by faith to the borders of the realm invisible, pass from the seen into the unseen world.

Moreover, faith shall merge into knowledge. Great fundamental facts and truths which we have received by faith on the authority of Christ, being beyond our ability to comprehend here, will grow luminous in the light of God's presence, and will pass into the realm of our understanding. "Now we see in a mirror, darkly; but then face to face." Knowledge in part shall give place to perfect knowledge. Then, in the light of this wider knowledge, we shall know the meaning of many things that confound our intellects here, and, among others, the mystery of human suffering.

Prayer

O you who dwells in light unapproachable, and in whom there is no darkness, hear my prayer, for I am one of your earth-born children enveloped in the mists and shadows of time and sense. I cannot understand all your dealings with me. O help me to trust you where I cannot trace you. Give me grace, heavenly Father, to bear whatever burdens it seems good to you to lay upon me. In my shortsightedness, I would always choose for myself prosperity, and freedom from life's pains and sorrows. But you know what is best for each of your children. If in the midst of earthly enjoyments and successes, my soul is weaned from you, and I lose my hold on things spiritual, and set my affections unduly on things earthly and temporal, do your in mercy draw me closer to you, and if it be a cross which you send to draw me back to you, help me still to sing,

"Nearer, my God, to Thee,
   Nearer to Thee;
   E'en though it be a cross
   That raiseth me."

May your Holy Spirit so enlighten my understanding, and so quicken my spiritual apprehension, that I may never forget your name is Love, and that your are my Father, and hence far more deeply concerned for my salvation than I can possibly be for those that I most love. Grant, most gracious Father, that your chastening rod may always serve to bring me closer to you, as you intend it. Help me to realize that the loss of any earthly good that results in spiritual gain is a blessing in disguise. I would rather be your child, chastened and disciplined by your loving hand, than to enjoy the ease and prosperity of the wicked. By whatever way seems good to you, whether in sunshine or shadow, on the heights of prosperity, or in the lowly vale of obscurity, do you, O Father, lead me on, so that I may at least reach your presence, see your face, and be transformed into the image of your dear Son. And to Father, Son and Holy Spirit, will we ascribe the praise for our salvation forevermore. Amen!

14. The Model Prayer

Our Father, who art in heaven, Hallowed be thy Name. Thy king-
dom come. Thy will be done on earth, as it is in heaven. Give us this day
our daily bread. And forgive us our trespasses, as we forgive those who
trespass against us. And lead us not into temptation; but deliver us from
evil: For thine is the kingdom, and the power, and the glory, forever and
ever. Amen!

What a marvelous prayer this is, in its scope, in its simplicity, in its sublimity, in its adaptation to human
needs! The more we study it, the more wonderful it will
appear in all these characteristics.

Our Father.

A volume could not tell us so much of the nature of God
as this simple phrase. It enters at once into the sphere of
human experience and appeals to the heart with tremen-
dous power. God is our Father! With what loving confidence, then, may we approach him! How deep and tender,
then, must be his concern for us, his earthly children! How
closely it draws all the human family together, for he is our
common Father! "The sky is the roof of but one family."
Divine Fatherhood, human brotherhood—what glorious

conceptions! How the world is being changed by them! We are not orphans, then, drifting about on the chance currents of time, without a purpose or a destiny, but we have a divine Father, who is guiding all things for the welfare of his children. For this sublime thought, in its fullness and tenderness, we are indebted to Jesus of Nazareth, who taught us this prayer.

Who art in heaven.

There is, then, a heaven, the home of God. But if it be God's home, it is our home also, for he is our Father. Where should the children be but in the Father's house? "In my Father's house are many mansions," said Jesus. "I go to prepare a place for you, and if I go and prepare a place for you, I will come again and receive you unto myself, that where I am there you may be also" (John 14:2,3). A heavenly Father and a heavenly home! Could words be more full of comfort!

Hallowed be your name.

Let the holy character of God be honored as holy, both with our lips and in our lives. If God our Father be holy, how holy, too, ought we, his children, to be, in all manner of conversation. Let us pray to be preserved from a careless and irreverent use of the name of the infinite and adorable Being whom we may call "Our Father," and in all things seek to be like him.

Your kingdom come.

This is the missionary spirit, breathing out its petition for the prevalence of God's reign over the lives of men. This will always be an appropriate petition for the disciples of Jesus, until the "last enemy shall be destroyed," and Christ shall transfer the kingdom to his Father, "that God may be all in all." True, it has already come to the earth, in its beginning, and has made much progress; but to a large part of the race, the kingdom of God has not yet come. A majority of the vast number of human beings who dwell upon the earth today know little or nothing of the kingdom of God. And even in Christian lands, how many there be who have never yielded to the authority of Christ. And of those who profess citizenship in the kingdom of God, how few, comparatively, have yielded their whole lives, with all their powers and talents to the service of God. It is evident, therefore, that we may still pray, "Your kingdom come." But if we *only* pray, and do nothing else to extend the kingdom of God throughout the world, we are falling far short of our duty, and are denying in our lives the prayer we utter with our lips. Every disciple of the Master is under the most solemn obligations to do what lies in his power, to hasten the time when "all the kingdoms of this world shall become the Kingdom of our Lord and of his Christ."

Your will be done on earth as it is in heaven.

This opens up a glorious vista of progress for the human race here in the world. The will of God is yet to be done on earth as it is in heaven. What a wonderful change does this involve! No more war nor bloodshed. No more strife and unholy rivalry between nations and individuals. No oppression of the poor by the rich, nor envy of the rich by the poor. No more saloons in the land, producing drunkards, orphans, widows, poverty, disgrace and crime. No more dishonesty, lying, unchastity, theft, murder, malice or hatred, for all shall be brothers and each shall seek his neighbor's welfare. This earth, then, will be an annex to heaven, and there will be "a new heaven and a new earth wherein dwelleth righteousness." Glorious era! Let us labor for it, and pray for it, that we may share in its everlasting joys.

Give us this day our daily bread.

Here is the beautiful spirit of dependence on, and trust in, a Father's love and care. When we can recognize all our daily blessings as gifts from the hand of our heavenly Father, the gratitude we feel will express itself in constant thanksgiving to him. It is not bread for a year that is asked for, but *daily* bread. This implies daily communion with God. Nor is it bread for the body only, that we need to ask God for, but for our spirit's daily food which he alone can supply. But neither in our petition for material nor for spiritual bread, may we omit the necessary effort on our part to secure these blessings. God confers his gifts upon us in the way that will be most profitable to us, and that is, through our own efforts, we working with God and he with us, and in us. Thus in cooperation with God do we obtain temporal and spiritual blessings.

And forgive us our trespasses as we forgive those who trespass against us.

The dear Lord knew our human weakness, and has taught, us how to pray for forgiveness. There must, of course, first of all, be a recognition of our sins, then sorrow for them and an earnest purpose to turn away from them. We must possess, too, the spirit of forgiveness, if we would be forgiven. If we do not forgive those who have trespassed against us neither will our heavenly Father forgive our trespasses. This is because the unforgiving spirit is an impenitent spirit, and therefore in no condition to receive forgiveness.

And lead us not into temptation, but deliver us from evil.

Here is the wise spirit of caution. This petition indicates a wholesome fear of sin, amid, what is all too uncommon, a recognition of our own weakness. The self-confident never utter this petition, except in a merely formal way. They do not feel the need of caution, and rush thoughtlessly into the midst of temptation, to find themselves unprepared to meet it. The temptations that lie in the path of duty are quite enough to test our faith and loyalty, without going out of our way to associate with the ungodly, and come under their vile influence. In the way of duty we may confidently rely on God's assistance, but in meeting self-chosen temptations, which we fund by walking in the way of transgressors, we have forfeited divine aid, and become an easy prey for the enemy of our souls. Evil is the one thing to be feared, and we do well to ask our heavenly Father to "deliver us from evil"—the evil that is without, and the evil thoughts that may arise within our own hearts. God alone can deliver us from the dominion of evil or the "Evil One. "

For thine is the kingdom, and the power, and the glory, forever and ever. Amen!

Although this doxology is not in the Revised Version, nor in several of the ancient manuscripts, it is supported by preponderating evidence from the Greek Fathers, and forms a fitting conclusion to this remarkable prayer. It is an ascription of praise to him before whom the heart has humbled itself in prayer, and expresses the natural outflowing of every loving and loyal citizen of the kingdom of God.

To *say*, or merely *repeat* such a prayer as the foregoing, grand as it is, means little; but to *pray* it, intelligently and sincerely, means very much. No one can do it habitually without growing into the likeness of Christ, out of whose heart it flowed. I would commend it for daily use, either alone, or as the conclusion of another prayer.

Scriptural Instructions for Prayer

Thus says the Lord, The heaven is my throne and the earth is my footstool: Where is the house that you built unto me and where is the place of my rest? For all those things my hand made, and all these have been, says the Lord. But to this man will I look; even to him that is poor and of a contrite spirit, and trembles at my word.

Be careful for nothing; but in every thing by prayer and supplication with thanksgiving, let your requests be made known unto God.

Seek the Lord, and his strength; seek his face continually.

Seek the Lord while he may be found; call upon him while he is near.

Continue in prayer, and watch in the same with thanksgiving. My brethren, be strong in the Lord, and in the power of his might.

Praying always with all prayer and supplication in the spirit; and watching with all perseverance.

Every good gift and every perfect gift is from above, and comes down from the Father of lights, with whom is no variableness, neither shadow of turning.

For the same Lord over all is rich unto all that call upon

him; for whoever shall call upon the name of the Lord shall be saved.

As for me, I will call upon God, and the Lord shall save me. Evening, and morning, and at noon, will I pray, and cry aloud, and he shall hear my voice.

I will cry unto God most high, unto God that performs all things for me.

For you, Lord, are good, and ready to forgive, and plenteous in mercy unto all them that call upon you.

The Lord is near unto all them that call upon him, to all that call upon him in truth.

He will fulfill the desire of them that fear him; he also will hear their cry, and will save them.

Draw near to God, and he will draw near to you: cleanse your hands, you sinners; and purify your hearts, you double-minded.

The Lord is far from the wicked, but he hears the prayer of the righteous.

If you abide in me, and my word abides in you, you shall ask what you will, and it shall be done unto you.

The eyes of the Lord are upon the righteous; and his ears are open unto their cry.

The righteous cry, and the Lord hears and delivers them out of all their troubles.

Acquaint now yourself with him, and be at peace.

For then shall you have your delight in the Almighty. You shall make your prayer unto him, and he shall hear you.

And when you stand praying, forgive, if you have anything against any; that your Father also which is in heaven may forgive you your trespasses.

For if you forgive men their trespasses, your heavenly Father will also forgive you: but if you forgive not men their trespasses, neither will your Father forgive your trespasses.

Say not, I will do so to him as he hath done to me: I will render to the man according to his work.

But love your enemies; bless them that curse you; do good to them that hate you; and pray for them that despitefully use you and persecute you; that you may be the children of your Father which is in heaven: for he makes his sun to rise on the evil, and on the good; and sends rain on the just, and on the unjust.

Be you therefore merciful, as your Father also is merciful.

If you deal your bread to the hungry; and that you bring the poor that are cast out to your house; when you see the naked, that you cover him; and that you hide not yourself from your own flesh. Then shall you call, and the Lord will answer; you shall cry, and he shall say, "Here I am."

But whoever stops his ears at the cry of the poor, he shall also cry himself, but shall not be heard.

I will therefore that men pray everywhere, lifting up holy hands without wrath and doubting.

And what things you desire when you pray, believe that you receive them, and you shall have them.

These things have I written unto you that believe in the name of the Son of God, that you may know that you have eternal life, and that you may believe on the name of the Son of God. And thus is the confidence that we have in him, that, if we ask anything according to his will, he hears us: and if we know that he hears us, whatsoever we ask, we know that we have the petitions that we desire of him.

If any of you lack wisdom, let him ask of God; that gives to all men liberally, and upbraids not, and it shall be given him: but let him ask in faith, nothing wavering; for he that wavers is like a wave of the sea, driven with the wind and tossed. For let not that man think that he shall receive anything of the Lord.

For you have not received the spirit of bondage again to fear; but you have received the spirit of adoption, whereby we cry, Abba, Father.

He that spared not his own Son, but delivered him up for us all, how shall he not with him also freely give us all things?

In whom we have boldness and access with confidence by the faith of him.

For there is one God, and one mediator between God and man, the man Jesus Christ, who give himself a ransom for all.

We have not an high priest which cannot be touched with the feeling of our infirmities; but was in all points tempted like as we are, yet without sin: let us therefore come boldly unto the throne of grace, that we may obtain mercy, and find grace to help in time of need.

Verily, verily, I say unto you, whatsoever you shall ask the Father in my name, he will give it you: hitherto have you asked nothing in my name: ask, and you shall receive, that your joy may be full.

And whatsoever you shall ask in my name, that will I do, that the Father may be glorified in the Son. If you shall ask anything in my name, I will do it.

Ask, and it shall be given you; seek, and you shall find; knock, and it shall be opened unto you; for every one that asks, receives; and he that seeks, finds; and to him that knocks, it shall be opened.

If you, then, being evil, know how to give good gifts unto your children; how much more shall your heavenly Father give the Holy Spirit to them that ask him?

Likewise the Spirit also helps our infirmities: for we know not what we should pray for as we ought: but the Spirit itself makes intercession for us with groanings which cannot be uttered: and he that searches the hearts knows what is the mind of the Spirit, because he makes intercession for the saints according to the will of God.

Let us lift up our hearts with our hands unto God in the heavens.

Fervent in spirit, serving the Lord: continuing instant in prayer.

We do not present our supplications before you for our righteousness; but for your great mercies O Lord, hear; O Lord, forgive; O Lord, hear, and do; defer not, for your own sake, O my God.

Let the words of any mouth and the meditation of my heart, be acceptable in your sight, O Lord, my strength and my redeemer.

PART II

FORMS OF PRAYER

FOR

I. PRIVATE DEVOTIONS.

II. FAMILY WORSHIP.

But thou, when thou prayest, enter into your closet, and when thou shut your door pray to your Father which is in secret and your Father, which seeth in secret, shall himself reward thee openly.

- JESUS

We feeble mortals have the privilege of speaking to our Maker. We utter words here, or pour out our desires in the closet, or when walking in the street or engaged in our daily employment we breathe an ejaculation. The word may be scarcely louder than a whisper, it may be inaudible to our neighbor and, yet it cannot die way into silence, nor can it be lost hrough blending with other sounds; nothing can drown it or prevent it from reaching its destination. It passes beyond sun and stars; it enters the presence-chamber of the Almighty. Amid the ceaseless strains of praise, that whisper reaches the divine ear, touches the infinite heart, moves the omnipotent arm. It sets in motion long trains of events, and brings down showers of blessings on those who utter it.

- W. LANDELS

PRIVATE DEVOTIONS

For Spiritual Renewal

Heavenly Father, renew me in the spirit of my mind, in my thoughts, my words, and life. May old sins pass away and all things be made new in one. May my affections be reclaimed to your service, that I may love you with all my heart, and my neighbor as myself. I have no sufficiency in myself; my sufficiency is in you. Knowing your will concerning me is my sanctification, may I earnestly and constantly strive to love you more and serve you better all the days of my life; through Christ our Lord. Amen!

For God's Blessing

O God, who has taught us to cast all our care on you, because you care for us, bless, I beseech you, my labor, my occupation, my friends and relatives, my worldly goods and possessions, that, being free from all undue care and anxiety concerning this present life, and setting my affections on things above, I may this day serve you, cheerfully, and help my neighbors readily to your honor and glory; for the love of Jesus Christ, your Son, our Lord. Amen!

For Spiritual Progress
(Lord's Day)

O Glorious Lord and Savior, who on the first day of the week did rise from the dead, and who is the resurrection and the life, I heartily beseech you to raise me, by true repentance and living faith, from the death of sin to the life of righteousness. Make this day a blessing to my soul that I may worship you, in spirit and in truth; that I may go to your house to be joyful and glad in you; that I may listen to my duty with an honest heart in order to practice it; and grant that the services of this day, both at home and at church, may fit me more for that rest that remains for the people of God; so that I and they may at length see your face in peace. In Christ's name. Amen!

For Spiritual Joy

A lmighty God, the redeemer and comforter of mankind, who, by your Holy Spirit, has prepared far greater pleasures than the world knows of for such as refuse the false pleasures of the world for your sake, tempering the troubles of this world with inward and secret solaces, to the intent that, being cheered and refreshed, we should run to you with gladder hearts; grant that the anointing of your Holy Spirit may cheer my mind with healthful gladness, that I may always serve you with a joyful heart; through Jesus Christ our Lord. Amen!

For Contrition

O Lord who despises not a contrite heart, and forgets the sins and wickedness of a sinner, in what hour he does mourn and lament his manner of living; grant unto me true contrition of heart, that I may truly condemn my sinful life past, and be wholly converted unto you; by our Lord and Savior Jesus Christ. Amen!

For Strength

O Lord, who told us to watch and pray that we enter not into temptation, give me, I beseech you, such strong desire to please you, that knowing the weakness of my mortal nature, I may flee with all my might from everything which may tempt me to offend against you, our loving Father; this I beg for the sake of your dear Son, Jesus Christ our Lord. Amen!

For Rulers

G od, whose kingdom rules over all, I pray for your blessing on all who have authority in Church or State; that by their wise and good administration of the laws, and our careful obedience to the same, I and all people may lead a quiet and peaceable life in all godliness and honesty; through your Son our Lord. Amen!

Confession of Sin

A t the close of this day, O heavenly Father, I confess my sins, my imperfections, and infirmities. I have sinned in thought, in speech, in act. (Specify them.) I am not worthy to be called your son. If you, Lord, should be extreme to mark what I have done amiss, I could not abide it. But have mercy upon me according to your loving kindness. Cast me not away from your presence. Take not your Holy Spirit from me; but grant that by his holy inspiration I may think and speak those things that are good; and by your grace perform the same this day and all the days of my life; through Jesus Christ. Amen!

For Obedience

A lmighty God, teach me to submit to the easy yoke of our Savior, Christ, and to take upon me his light burden. Incline me unto all holy obedience to your will. May my heart be so rooted and grounded in your love, that no difficulties may discourage me in the way of well doing; and that neither the cares nor pleasures of life may lead me astray from you. Increase in me that which is lacking; raise up in me that which is fallen; restore to me that which I have lost; quicken in me that which may be ready to die; so that I may serve and obey you in all things; through Jesus Christ our Lord. Amen!

For Holy Living

Almighty God, as you promised to give your Holy Spirit to them that ask you, I humbly pray for this gift, that I may be kept from carelessness of spirit and hardness of heart; from fretfulness and impatience; from vanity and pride; from irreverence and indevotion; from repining at your dispensations and neglecting your warnings; and from all sin and wickedness. Give to one such love and joy and peace and long-suffering and gentleness and faith and meekness and temperance, that I may daily crucify the flesh, with its affections and lusts. And this I beg for Jesus Christ's sake. Amen!

For Right Living

Grant, O heavenly Father, that I may live this day as your child. Give me resolution to deny all sinful inclinations; to subdue all corrupt affections; to take revenge for my intemperance by mortification; for misspending my time by retirement; for the errors of my tongue by silence; for all the sins of my life by deep humility and repentance. And while penitent for my sins, may I be joyful and glad in you, so that by the brightness of my life and the cheerfulness of my conversation, I may commend the religion and church of Christ to all I converse with; through Jesus Christ, our Lord. Amen!

For Purity

Blessed Lord, who redeemed us unto God by your blood and consecrated all the people to be temples of the Holy Spirit, make me a fit dwelling place for your Spirit. Cast out of me everything that defiles; all impure lusts, sinful affections, covetous desires, vain imaginations, and everything contrary to your holy will, that I may serve you this day with a pure and humble mind; through Jesus Christ our Lord. Amen!

For Our Neighbors

Soften my heart, O Lord, that I may be moved at the necessities and griefs of others. O most mild and merciful Christ, I beseech you, breathe upon me the Spirit of your meekness and goodness; that like as your pity made you to endure most bitter death for us, so my pitying of them may lead me to succor all those who need it, and to the uttermost of my power; for your name's sake. Amen!

For Others

Lord, I pray for the church, that it may grow like Christ; for the world, that it may be turned to you; for my native land, that it may be governed after your will; for my family, my kinsmen according to the flesh, my friends, and enemies if I have any, that all may partake of your grace here and of your glory hereafter; through our Lord and Savior Jesus Christ. Amen!

Thanksgiving

Almighty God and heavenly Father, who of your gracious providence and tender mercy preserved me, I humbly praise and magnify your glorious name for all your goodness to me this day. If I have walked uprightly and honestly and truthfully; if I have kept my tongue as with a bridle, it is of your mercy, O Lord, my God; therefore thanks and praise be to you this night; through Jesus Christ. Amen!

Against Spiritual Sloth

God, our heavenly Father, give me such a measure of your grace that, forgetting those things which are behind, and reaching forth unto those things which are before, I may press toward the mark for the prize of the high calling of God in Christ

Jesus; to whom, with you and the Holy Spirit, be honor and glory, world without end. Amen!

For Knowledge

Lord Jesus, who is a living fountain to them that know you, perpetual food to them that hunger after you, glory to them that seek you, joy to them that find you; may I seek and find and know you, as the one only and everlasting good, in whom are pardon and peace and everlasting felicity now and for ever. Amen!

For Mercy

Have mercy upon me, O God, after your great goodness; according to the multitude of your mercies do away with my offences. Wash me thoroughly from my wickedness and cleanse me from my sin. I acknowledge my faults and my sins are ever before me, Against you only have I sinned and done evil in your sight. You shall purge me with hyssop, and I shall be clean; you shall wash me, and I shall be whiter than snow; you shall make me hear of joy and gladness, that the bones which you have broken may rejoice. Turn your face away from my sins, and blot out all my misdeeds. Make me a clean heart, O God, and renew a right spirit within me. Cast me not away from your presence, and take not your Holy Spirit from me. Amen!

Confession

O Lord, our heavenly Father, merciful and gracious, long-suffering and abundant in goodness and in truth; I call to mind your exceeding love in having redeemed me with the precious blood of Christ, lest the consciousness of my sins should drive me to despair. I know I have sinned in thought, in word, in deed. (Make mention of your sins.) Lord, make me truly penitent, that I may abhor myself for the sins I have committed, and turn unto you with full purpose to lead a sober, righteous, and godly life; through Jesus Christ. Amen!

Commendatory

As I go forth to the duties of this day, remembering the snares and trials and temptations which await me, I commend myself to you, O Lord, humbly asking that your grace may help me, your mercy defend me, and your good Spirit aid me, so that I may not yield to sin; for the glory of your name; through Jesus Christ our Lord. Amen!

For Perserverance

Give me grace, O Lord, to lay aside every weight and the sin which does so easily beset me, to run with patience the race that is set before me, looking unto Jesus, the Author and Finisher of our faith, who for the joy that was set before him, endured the cross, despising the shame, and is set down at the right hand of the throne of God. Amen!

For Grace

O Lord God, remove from me all iniquity, superstition, and hypocrisy; all haughtiness, strife and wrath; all indolence and fraud; all lying and injuriousness; every evil notion, impure thought, and base desire. Grant me to be truly religious and godly; give me patience and a good temper; purity and soberness; contentment and truth, with perseverance in all good to the end; through Jesus Christ. Amen!

For Pardon

O merciful Lord and God, I have sinned, but I do not hide my sins, for I have confessed them before you. Forgive them not for my own merits or goodness, but for the merits and worthiness of our Lord Jesus Christ, who died, the just for the unjust, that he might bring us unto you. For the sake of his atonement upon the cross, may all my sins be blotted out, so that I may serve you acceptably, and at last attain eternal life with you; and to you shall be all the praise now and forever. Amen!

For the Holy Spirit

O blessed Lord, who promised to give your Holy Spirit to them that ask you, and are more willing to bestow this gift than I to ask for it, give me the increase of your heavenly Spirit, that he may bear witness with my spirit that I am your child and heir of your kingdom; and that by the operation of His grace, I may kill all my carnal lusts and evil affections contrary to your will; for the worthiness of your Son. Amen!

For Meekness

L ord Jesus, who when you were reviled did not revile again; when you suffered did not threaten, but did commit yourself to him who judges righteously; give me the like spirit of meekness and patience, that I may repress all wrath, strife, murmuring, malice, and envy; that I may refrain from all peevish dispositions and from that unevenness of spirit which hinders me from the discharge of duty and from giving pleasure to those around me; I ask these blessings for your name's sake. Amen!

Intercession

C all to mind this day, O Lord, before you, all who are near and dear to me; beseeching you to remember them for good, and to supply their desires and wants as may be most expedient for them. To those in sickness and sorrow, grant relief; to those tempted, bestow deliverance; to those careless, give repentance; to those in doubt, give assurance. And with all honesty of desire, I commend to your mercy all who have wronged me by word or deed, beseeching you to forgive them all their sins, and to bring them with me to your heavenly kingdom; through Christ our Lord. Amen!

For Right Living

Almighty God, who knows I am weak and tempted and easily led into sin, help me to walk uprightly and in your fear all the days of my life. Make me pure in thought; truthful and kind in speech; honest and upright in my dealings with my fellowmen. Give me humility, that I be not vain; patience, that I be not angry; kindness to others, that I be not selfish. May I always live so as never to be afraid or unprepared to die; all this, through Jesus Christ our Lord. Amen!

Confession

O Lord God, I would make humble and honest confession of my sins to you this night. You have comforted us by saying, if we confess our sins, you are faithful and righteous to forgive them. I know that though I have confessed you with my tongue, I have oftentimes denied you by my acts. My eyes have been often opened to let in sin; my ears have been often ready to receive sinful discourse; I have let loose my tongue; I have yielded my members as instruments of sin; I lave defiled my heart by vain and foolish and impure imaginations; I have wasted my time and have not lived answerably to my means of grace. If you, Lord, should be extreme to mark what I have done amiss, I should have no hope. But there is mercy with you; let your mercy rest upon me now, henceforth and forever; for Jesus Christ's sake. Amen!

For God's Care for the Day

Spared to see another day in health and peace, before going forth to my appointed work, I commend myself to the God and Father of our Lord Jesus Christ; beseeching him to keep me from all sin and danger, that I may live as in his presence and be joyful and glad in him all this day. In Jesus' name, Amen!

For Trust

Almighty God, who never fails them who put their trust in you, help me to put all my trust in you, and you alone. In all difficulties may I have recourse to you; in all troubles to rest and depend upon you. You will keep him in perfect peace whose mind is stayed on you; let me stay myself upon you, that you who are the confidence of all the ends of the earth, may be my confidence forever. I would commit myself to the ordering of your providence, so as to lie anxious for nothing, but always to be of the number of your faithful children. Grant me this abiding trust; through Christ our Lord. Amen!

For Strength to Resist Temptation

O Lord, you who are the refuge of all who put their trust in you, I am weak, but you are strong. Give me, of your strength, to resist temptation, and especially the sin that does so easily beset me. O Lord, you know my weakness. My hope is in you. Deliver me, O Lord, from all practices that are injurious to myself in body, or spirit, and displeasing to you. Help me to be obedient to your will, and to say, from my heart, "Not my will, O Lord, but yours be done!" Help me to avoid temptation, and do not allow me to be tempted above that I am able to bear. O my Father! take my heart and mould it after your likeness. Take my life and use it to your glory. Lead me to do and suffer your will here, and finally receive me through the merits of Jesus Christ, Our Lord. Amen!

A Young Convert's Prayer

Dear Lord, I am but a little child and know not how to go out or come in. Teach me how to pray. You know that I love you and that I need your divine guidance in all things. you are my Father and I am your child. As you brought me into this sweet and holy relation to yourself, will you not so direct me that I shall walk worthy of you unto all pleasing? O give me light and strength for the new life upon which I have entered that I may ever pursue the straight and narrow way. Feed me with the heavenly manna. Gird me with your everlasting arm. Shelter me under the shadow of your wing. Fold me to your loving breast. Fill me with your Holy Spirit. Help me to abide in you as the branch abides in the vine. Give me daily a deeper and more vital union with yourself, and grant that I may never lose the blessed consciousness that you are mine and that I am yours.

My Father, you know the fierce temptations which assail me and by which, alas, I have been so often led astray. O pity my infirmities. Forgive my shortcomings and transgressions. Perfect your strength in my weakness. Uphold me with your Almighty hand. And, dear Lord, so fortify me with your grace that I shall be able always to resist the tempter and to fulfill my vows to you.

Help me to grow in grace and in divine knowledge. Sanctify to my good every ministry of your gospel and every trial of my experience, that day by day I may be purer, stronger, braver, truer, better, than before. Increase my zeal and power as a worker in your vineyard. Make me a more active and useful member of your church. May my life abound in greater blessing to those around me. And may my upturned heart ever say to you, "Lord, what wilt you have *me* to do?"

Give me patience to run my race diligently to the end. May my heart never lose its first love. May my hands never weary in well doing. And may the precious hope of an endless life to come be the anchor of my soul, sure and steadfast, until the glad day when my earthly wanderings shall cease and you will bid me forever welcome to your heavenly home; and to you, through the blessed Jesus, shall be praises forever more. Amen!

In Time of Perplexity and Trouble

Almighty God, Our Heavenly Father! How often must we cry out with the psalmist, "Why art you cast down, O my soul, and why are you disquieted within me; hope in God!" We are burdened with life's increasing cares; temptations assail us; our enemies plot against us; a thousand untoward events transpire along our way, and vague fears haunt and disturb our souls. Friends we have trusted may have proven false, and our purest motives been misunderstood. We are cast down in spirit and are troubled on every side. Blessed Father, to whom can we go but to you? You are the refuge of all who put their trust in you. Help me to feel that behind these clouds which shadow my path, your face is still smiling upon me. Give me peace, O God, and help me to feel that the everlasting arms are beneath me. May I be enabled to cast all my fear and care upon you, and lie down and sleep in peace. Give me a faith that trusts you in the storm, and fears not. O receive and calm and soothe my troubled and perplexed spirit, you God of all comfort, through Jesus Christ our Lord! Amen!

For Increase of Faith

I believe Lord, help you my unbelief. Increase my faith. Help me to come into your presence, O God, with loving, child-like confidence, believing not only that you are, but that you are a rewarder of them who diligently seek you. Forbid that I should cherish any intellectual pride, or science falsely so called, that would prevent me from trusting in you with my whole heart, or hinder me from walking in your holy precepts. Keep me, I humbly beseech you, heavenly Father, from the dominion of those fleshly appetites and passions that war against the spirit and weaken faith. Help me to endure as seeing him who is invisible. Almighty God, I do humbly entreat you to so strengthen my faith in you, and in the spiritual realities of the unseen world, that if I shall be called upon to endure affliction, or to pass through the dark shadows of human sorrow, I may be enabled to walk by faith and trust you even when I cannot trace you. Help me to realize fully the precious truth that all things work together for good to them that love you and are called according to your purpose. May I be among those who are kept by the power of God, through faith, unto the salvation ready to be revealed in the last time, that, at life's close, I may say with your servant Paul, "I have kept the faith." And this I ask in Christ's name. Amen!

For Pardon

O Lord, hear my prayer, and attend unto the voice of my supplication. I have sinned against you and have done wickedly in your sight. My conscience testifies against me, and mine own heart condemns me. I acknowledge my transgression, O God, and beseech you, for Christ's sake, to blot out my iniquity. Purge me that I may be clean, wash me and I shall be whiter than snow. Not only do I seek your forgiveness, for my sin, but I would most humbly implore you, most merciful Father, to renew within me a right spirit of mind, by which I may henceforth loathe the sins I have committed. Like as a father pities his children, so, O Lord, you pity those that fear you, for you know our frame, that we are dust. Grant us, once more, the peace our sins have destroyed, and the joys of your salvation. Strengthen me by your Spirit, deliver me from temptation that I may not be able to bear, and glorify your name in and through me. For Christ's sake. Amen!

For Refuge in God

O Lord, you are our refuge in every time of trouble and of danger. Though we forget you, too often, when our path is unshadowed, and all goes well with us, yet in the day of affliction, when clouds overspread our sky, you are remembered by us as our only refuge, and to you we flee. Gracious Father, hear us, when we call upon you, and grant us your protection. Help me, dear Father, in the midst of distress and danger and care, to trust you more fully, and to commit myself to your care in filial confidence. May I be able to realize more fully than I have ever done that "all things work together for good to them that love God and are the called according to his purpose." Help me to feel that underneath me at all times are the everlasting arms. So shall I have peace and rest. Keep me, O Lord, under the shadow of your wings, until life's storms be over past, and bring me with all your faithful ones, to the peaceful haven of everlasting rest, through Jesus Christ, to whom be glory, forever and ever. Amen!

In Sickness

O you who are the fountain of life; in you we live and move and have our being. It has pleased you, in your providential government of the world, to afflict your children with sickness and disease at times. These are not accidents, but occur under a system of law of which you are the author. We believe these afflictions are intended for our good. Often by the chastisement of our bodies, our spirits are made purer. While it is necessary for me to bear this sickness, give me patience and meekness, and grant that I may be profited spiritually thereby. But if it be consistent with your will, restore me soon to health and strength, that I may perform my allotted work and do your will among men. Whatever may be the issue, grant me forgiveness of sin, and a sense of your nearness, and the grace to say, "Not my will but yours be done." We ask all in Christ's name. Amen!

Birthday

A lmighty God, the Father and Maker of all, things, whose blessed Providence has been over me ever since I was born, I praise and magnify your glorious name for your great goodness towards me, most humbly beseeching you that I may be taught to number my days, and to apply my heart unto wisdom, that I may know to what end both body and soul have been given unto me, even to serve you, the living God; that I may bewail my sinful years past, and spend the rest of my time here in godliness and righteousness; and that as I have now finished another year of my life here in your favor, so I may continue and finish up the remainder of my days in your fear, and you may at the Last Day raise me from the grave of this sorrowful earth, to live a new and glorious life with you forever, through Jesus Christ our Lord. Amen!

For the Love of God

O God, the God of all goodness and grace, who are worthy of a greater love than we can give or understand; fill my heart,

I beseech you, with such love toward you as may cast out all sloth and fear, that nothing may seem too hard to do or suffer in obedience to you; and grant that by thus loving, I may daily become more like unto you, and finally obtain the crown of life which you promised to those that love you; through Jesus Christ our Lord. Amen!

For Patience

O Almighty Father, give to your child a meek and gentle spirit, that I may be slow to anger, and easy to be entreated to forgiveness. Let me not be moved with every trifling mistake in the conversation and intercourse of others, and enable me not only to check my irritation, but to be so full of sympathy and loving-kindness, that I may not feel it. Teach me in all cases to remember what others feel, and, what they have a right to expect, and give grace, when I have been betrayed into fretfulness or irritation, to confess my fault, and patiently to bear the ill-will I may have occasioned. O my Savior, make me, I beseech you, like unto you, humble, loving, gentle and courteous; forgive me as I earnestly desire to forgive others; and grant that, having striven to serve you here, I may dwell with you forever hereafter, for your loving mercy's sake. Amen!

Prayer for Truth

O God, the God of truth, mercifully grant that the Holy Spirit of Truth may rule my heart, grafting therein love of truth, and making me in all my thoughts and words and works, to study, speak and follow truth, that I may be sincere before men, and blameless before you. May no unworthy prejudice or sectarian pride prevent me from accepting whatever bears the divine impress of your truth. May I love the truth, know the truth, and be made free by the truth; for His sake who is the Way, the Truth, and the Life, and in whom is no guile, even Jesus Christ our Lord. Amen!

For Temperance

OAlmighty Father, who bountifully provided for all our wants, preserve me from self-indulgence and excess in the use of all your bounties, and give me the spirit of temperance and sobriety, that in eating and drinking I may seek only to serve my necessity with moderation and thanksgiving, and not my pleasure. Grant me rather to hunger and thirst after righteousness, and so to keep under my body that my spirit may be always wakeful and ready for your service, and I may be found worthy to be admitted to the Eternal Supper of the Lamb; for his sake who hungered and thirsted for us, Jesus Christ our Lord. Amen!

Prayer for Christ-likeness

Our Heavenly Father, we thank you for all your loving kindness and tender mercy. We praise your name that you revealed yourself to us in Jesus Christ Our Savior. You have not left us in darkness and. despair; but you caused the light to shine upon us. You illuminated the pathway that leads from earth to heaven. Yea, you have shined into our hearts and filled us with light, and joy, and love. You led us out of darkness into light; out of despair into hope; out of sin into righteousness. Blessed be your holy name!

O what wondrous love you shown toward us in Jesus Christ our Lord! What could we do without Jesus? He has trodden life's pathway before us. He has shown us the perfect life. He has known the depths of human experience; and yet without sin. He has shown us how to be in the world, but not of the world. He has gone down into the valley and the shadow and parted the waters of death that we may go joyously over. He has ascended to the heavens, where he now pleads our cause before your throne.

Dear Father, help us to become more and more like him. O may we be made partakers of the Divine Nature, escaping the corruption of the world through lust. We long for Christ to be formed in us, the hope of glory; for if we are like him here we know we shall be like him hereafter; for we shall see him as he is.

When we stand in the presence of the matchless life of Jesus, we feel so keenly the sense of our unworthiness. There seems such a gulf, wide and deep, separating us from him. Help us, our Father, to so live that, as we grow in years, we may grow toward him. May we become purer in heart, holier in life, more God-like in nature, more Christ-like in disposition.

And when we will have reached the end of our pilgrimage; when the last battle will have been fought and the last victory will have been won, may our blessed Savior take us by the hand, and say, "Well done; come up higher."

Now unto God our Father, be the praise and the glory, through Jesus Christ our Lord. Amen!

During an Absence from Home

Almighty God, who knows all my weakness far better than it is known to me, remember me now and visit me with your grace, lest in the company of strangers, and amid many new things, my heart be stolen away from you, and be inclined to evil. Prepare me, I beseech you, for whatever the day may bring forth. Hold me up and I shall be safe. Let me never forget that I am your servant, and that you are my God. Give me grace to abstain from all appearance of evil; and of your great mercy grant that the souls of your people may never be hurt by my words or my example, but rather may be edified, to the honor and praise of your name; through Jesus Christ our blessed Lord and Savior. Amen!

For the Use of Wealth

O Lord, whose is the earth and the fullness thereof, all we have we have derived from you. You committed to my care and stewardship more earthly possessions than to many others of your servants. Help me to realize that my ownership of these goods is not absolute, but that I and all I have belong to you. Give me grace and wisdom to so use the means in my possession as to honor your name and bless humanity. Forbid that I should set my heart on earthly riches and neglect the true wealth of the soul. Give me a liberal heart, that I may so consecrate what I have to your cause that it may not testify against me in the last day. If at any time you see that my possessions are a hindrance to my soul's progress, and a peril to my salvation, then, O Father, remove them from me and give them to others who can more wisely use them. Help me and all others to whom you have given riches to be rich in good works, to be humble-minded, just to those in our service, ready to distribute, willing to communicate to the necessities of others. May we be zealous in laying up our treasures in heaven, where neither moth nor rust corrupt and where thieves do not break through nor steal. And when heart and flesh shall fail us, receive us, we beseech you, into everlasting habitations, through riches of grace in Christ Jesus, our Lord. Amen!

For Love to Others

Almighty Father, who promised to forgive us even as we ourselves forgive; fill me, I beseech you, with such intense love towards you, that loving my friends in you, my enemies for you, I may obtain your promises, and be made a partaker of your heavenly kingdom; through our Lord Jesus Christ. Amen!

Before a Journey

O Lord, save me, your servant, for I put my trust in you. Grant to me, O my God, a prosperous journey this day. May your loving care be with me to protect me in all dangers of body or of soul. Guide me on my way to the place whither I would go; grant me to return to my home in health and safety; and when life's journey is ended, bring me to my rest in Paradise, and finally to the glory of your Eternal Kingdom, for the sake of my merciful Savior. Amen!

After a Safe Return

Thank you, O Lord, that it hath pleased you to restore me, your servant, in peace and safety to my home. Give me due thankfulness, I beseech you, for this and all your favors, and grant that, through every dispensation of your Providence, whether for sorrow or for joy, I may acquire a more sure trust in your mercy, and a more comfortable hope of everlasting life; through Jesus Christ our Lord. Amen!

For Our Parents

Almighty God, who strictly commanded us to honor our father and our mother next unto you, grant me of your goodness and grace so to love and honor my parents, to fear and to obey them, as you in your Holy Word directed and charged me to do; that both in their life and at their death their souls may bless me, and by your fatherly mercy I may obtain that blessing which you promised to those that honor their father and their mother; and that you, seeing my unfeigned heart and reverence toward them, may become my loving, heavenly Father, and number me among those your children, who are heirs of your glorious kingdom; through your well beloved and dear Son, Jesus Christ our Lord. Amen!

For Absent Friends

O God, who is everywhere present, let your loving mercy and compassion rest on the head of your servants now absent from us. May your holy angels guard them; your Holy Spirit guide them; your Providence minister to their necessities. Let your blessing be on them night and day. Sanctify them in their bodies, souls, and spirit. Keep them unblamable to the coming of Christ, and make us all to dwell with you forever, in the light of your Countenance and in your Glory, for our dear Lord's sake. Amen!

For One who has Asked our Prayers in Trouble

Almighty and Everlasting God, Comfort of the sorrowful, Strength of the weary, our only Help in time of need, may the prayers of all that call upon you in trouble, and especially the prayers of your servant, come into your Presence, that he may rejoice evermore in your merciful aid and deliverance, through Jesus Christ our Lord. Amen!

For Diligence in Work

O God, who commanded that we should always work with our hands the thing that is good, give me grace that I may diligently do my duty in that state of life to which it has pleased God to call me. May I honestly strive to improve the talents committed to my care, and grant that no worldly business, no worldly pleasure, may ever divert me from the thought of the world to come; through Jesus Christ our Lord. Amen!

Against Evil Thoughts

O Eternal God mercifully regard my prayers, and deliver my heart from the temptation of wicked thoughts, that I may be the Temple of the Holy Spirit. Forbid that I should cherish unholy thoughts in my heart, until they ripen into acts of disobedience, and so produce death. Help me to keep my heart pure; that I may see you and dwell with you forever, through Christ our Lord. Amen!

For Ministers of the Gospel

O Lord, my God and Savior, the Guide and Shepherd of your flock, hear, I beseech you, the prayer which I would now offer unto you, in behalf of those whom you ordained to be the pastors of your people, the ministers of your Church.

Look down upon them, O Lord, in mercy; enlighten those who are in perplexity; uphold those that stand; raise up those who are falling away; arouse the negligent; strengthen the penitent; comfort those who are in affliction; support those who are laboring amidst difficulties and privations, especially such as are ministering in foreign lands; and give to all a firm faith in your revelation; zeal, and wisdom, in making it known; and an ever-present sense of their awful responsibility; that so they may be faithful stewards of your mysteries and diligent dispensers of your Holy Word here, and may be finally accepted in that Great Day when they shall be called to answer at your Judgment Seat for the souls

entrusted to their charge. Grant this, O Lord, my Redeemer, of
your great mercy. Amen!

For the Grace of Love

O Lord, who taught us that all our doings without charity are
nothing worth; shed abroad in our hearts by your Holy
Spirit, that most excellent gift of charity, the very bond of peace
and of all virtues, without which whosoever lives is counted dead
before you. May this grace of love enable us to live together in
unity, in peace, and in kindly and helpful intercourse, each
esteeming others better than himself, and in honor preferring one
another. Grant this for your only Son Jesus Christ's sake. Amen!

For Trust in Time of Anxiety

O most loving Father, who wills us to give thanks for all
things, to dread nothing but the loss of you, and to cast all
our cares on you, who cares for us; preserve us from faithless
fears and worldly anxieties, and grant that no clouds of this mortal life may hide from us the light of that love which is immortal,
and which you manifested to us in your Son Jesus Christ our
Lord. You know, dear Father, the burden of our hearts, which is
too great for us. So strengthen our faith that we may cast our burden upon you, and cause the events that now distress us, to work
for our eternal good; in Jesus' name. Amen !

For the Sucess of the Spoken Word

We beseech you to bless your word wherever spoken throughout the universal Church. Oh, make it a word of power and
peace, to convert those who are not yet yours, and to confirm those
that are. Particularly bless it in this our land, which you have made
a land of light, and a storehouse of your treasures and mercies. Oh,
let not our foolish and unworthy hearts rob us of the continuance
of this your sweet love; but pardon our sins, and perfect what you
began. Make your word a swift word, passing from the ear to the
heart, from the heart to the lip and conversation; that, as the rain

returns not empty, so neither may your word, but accomplish that for which it is given; through Jesus Christ our Lord. Amen!

For Those Who Preach the Word

O Lord, strengthen your ministers today that they may speak with power, and teach you those that are set to teach your people. Pour upon your churches the spirit of prayer, that not their lips only, but their hearts may speak unto you. Awaken the careless, convince the doubting, confirm the weak, add power to the strong. May every Lord's day prepare us for the Day of the Lord; and each time that we celebrate his resurrection, fit us to rise when he shall call us to glory; through Jesus Christ our Lord. Amen!

For Parents

O my Heavenly Father, who by your great mercy adopted me into your divine family, help me to be an obedient child. I thank you for Christian parents who early taught me the way of righteousness. You taught us in your word, to honor our parents. I pray for Divine help, O Lord, that I may so honor, love and respect my father and my mother, that I may never willingly do aught to give them pain, anxiety, or grief. Help me to be mindful of their deep and tender concern for my well being, and of all they have done for me, and seek to gladden their hearts, and smooth their rugged way in their declining years. Soon, alas, in the course of nature, they will be called hence, and I shall no more hear their prayers and counsels. While they are yet with me, O loving Father, help me to lighten their burdens, relieve their wants, and reverence their wishes, that when they are gone I may have no reason for self-reproach at the memory of any needless pain I have caused them. And this, in Jesus' name, Amen!

Before Going to the House of the Lord

O God, Father of our Lord Jesus Christ, who promised to be wherever two or three are gathered together in your name;

cleanse the thoughts of our hearts as we come to you in your house. Help us to cast out from our souls every evil feeling or desire; all envy, pride and hypocrisy, all falsehood, deceit, and worldly anxiety, all covetousness, vain-glory, and sloth, all malice, wrath, and anger, all remembrance of injuries, and every motion of the flesh and spirit contrary to your holy will, that, with freedom, without condemnation, with a pure and contrite heart, with sanctified lips, and without confusion of face, we may appear before you, boldly call upon your name, hear with all devotion your most holy Word, and worthily adore you, Father, Son, and Holy Spirit, one God, world without end. Amen!

For an Evening Devotion

Gracious Father, Giver of all good, we have enjoyed your blessing this day and come now to give you thanks. You have strewn our path with blessings and filled our hearts with delight. Harm has not approached us nor is there any visible mark of your displeasure upon us. You sent us air to breathe, water to quench our thirst, and we have been permitted to feed upon your bounty. Yet we confess our faults, and ask you for pardon, and for that grace that will keep us from the wrong and direct us in the right. We pray for protection during the night, and for strength and wisdom with which to begin the work of the coming day. Let your blessing rest upon every right deed and thought of this day, and remove the power for evil from every error. Help us to see in the closing day the emblem of the close of life that we may be as well prepared for that change as we are now to rest from the toils of the day. May we always trust in you, and be received into your presence with exceeding great joy at last. For Christ's sake. Amen!

In Preparation for Communion

O God, the Searcher of all hearts, prepare me, I beseech you, to receive, in a proper spirit of devotion, the sacred emblems of Christ's broken body and shed blood. Help me to be truly penitent for all my sins, and to discern, in the bread and the wine, the body and blood of the Lord Jesus by whose sacrifice I alone may hope for forgiveness. Forbid, O Lord, that I should approach this sacred feast in a thoughtless spirit and without an earnest desire and sincere purpose to henceforth walk more worthy of the vocation wherewith I have been called; in Christ's name. Amen!

Lord Jesus, I would draw near to you today, in the sacred ordinance that we are to observe in memory of you. Help me to come with a penitent heart, in charity with my neighbors, in peace with all my brethren, and with a full purpose to lead a better life, keeping your commandments and walking in your holy ways. Help me to so participate in this solemn, yet joyful feast, that I may be spiritually refreshed and enabled to serve you more acceptably, all my days. And to your blessed name, be present and everlasting praises world without end. Amen!

Almighty God, our gracious heavenly Father, as I am about to join with your children in the memorial feast of the Lord's Supper, in memory of Christ, who gave himself a ransom for us, grant that as I partake of the sacred emblems, I may reconsecrate myself to your service, and henceforth live more purely and unselfishly; for his dear name's sake. Amen!

Brief Prayers at Bedtime

O Lord, who never slumbers or sleeps, be pleased in your mercy to watch over me this night. Guard me while waking, and defend me while sleeping, that when I wake, I may watch with Christ, and when I sleep, I may rest in peace. Grant this favor for his sake, our only Savior and Redeemer. Amen!

Into your hands, O Lord, I commend myself, and all who are dear to me. Grant us to pass through this night without sin, and without fear; awaken us at the fitting time, the time of prayer, and grant us to rise and seek you early, to your glory and our eternal good. Amen!

Loving Savior, strength of the weary, rest of the restless, by the weariness and unrest of your sacred Cross, come to me who am weary, that I may rest in you. Amen!

O Lord, who did bid the winds and waves be still, lay your hand upon my head, and keep it still in you, as in a haven sheltered from the troubled sea. Amen!

Grant me, O Lord, above all things that can be desired, to rest in you, and in you to have my heart at peace. You are the true peace of the soul, you its only rest. Teach me to feel all things without you to be unsatisfying and restless. In this very peace, our one chiefest and eternal good, may I ever sleep and rest. Amen!

Lord, support me all the day long of this troublous life, until the shadows lengthen, and the evening comes, and the busy world is hushed, and the fever of life is over, and my work is done. Then, in your mercy, give me a safe lodging in Paradise, and a holy rest and peace at the last; through Jesus Christ our Lord. Amen!

For Use by Those at School

O God of all wisdom, grace and truth, I thank you that you have given me the desire for knowledge and some capacity for acquiring it. Help me to be faithful and diligent in all my studies, respectful and obedient to my teachers, gentle and courteous to my fellow students, and to strive so to behave myself as to be a good example for others. While I am seeking mental improvement, and that intellectual training that will fit me for my work in life, grant, I beseech you, heavenly Father, that I may not neglect my moral and spiritual culture, without which all knowledge is vain. Help me to keep in loving memory my parents to whom I am indebted for these privileges, and to cherish fondly the precepts and instruction I have received at their hand. Help me to compensate them in some measure for the anxiety and loneliness that my absence from home may occasion, by the manner in which I behave myself at school, and the progress I make in my studies.

O you great Teacher, who are meek and lowly in heart, will you assist me in all my efforts to improve my mind and strengthen my character in virtue, to the end that I may serve you acceptably here, and enjoy your presence forever. For your name's sake: Amen!

On Choosing a Vocation

Almighty God, our heavenly Father, we are glad that we may come to you with all questions that perplex us, and for the solution of which we feel our need of wisdom. As the time has come when I ought to choose my calling in life, I beseech you, in a special manner, to direct me aright. Help me to honestly and fearlessly examine my motives, and to be influenced only by those that are in harmony with your will. May it be my supreme desire, as a disciple of Christ, to pursue that calling in life in which I may do most to promote his cause and kingdom in the world. Help me to be willing, at all times, to follow what seems to be the leadings of your providence, and not to lean too much on my own understanding. Will you enable me to be faithful in whatever pursuit I may engage, and at last to receive your divine plaudit, "Well done, good and faithful servant." For Christ's Sake. Amen!

FAMILY WORSHIP

"Let prayer be the key of the morning and the bolt of the evening."

The family is a divine institution, and is older than the church or the state. In it, the material must be prepared out of which the church and state are built. Its purity, peace and order is of primary and fundamental importance, On the religious training of the young depends the well being of society and of the world. The momentous issues involved in the family would seem to make it the most reckless of experiments to attempt to rear the young without the purifying, restraining and molding influence of religion. The neglect of family worship, or irreligion in the home, has much to do with the deplorable lack of morality and religion among the young people of today. Let no family, where one or more of the parents pretend to be Christians, be without the daily worship. You may not see its beneficial effects on your children now, but the blessed influence of these hallowed hours will go with them, as they go out of the old home into the wide world, and will, in many an hour of sore temptation, strengthen and sustain them. The voices of father and mother, in reading the Blessed Volume, or in prayer to God, or the blended voices of the family, young and old, singing some sweet old melody of praise, will be wafted to them across the gulf of years, long after the parental voices have been hushed in death, and will bring before their minds the half-forgotten lessons and admonitions of long ago. But it is also a present blessing, being a most effective reinforcement of parental authority in securing obedience and order, and a powerful formative influence upon the character of the young. If you have hitherto, through timidity or other cause, neglected this most important part of your parental duty, we would urge you, in Christ's name, to neglect it no longer.

Resolve to begin at once. To assist you in so doing, has been our object in presenting these forms. A few brief hints as to the manner of conducting the home worship is all that our space will permit:

1. Let it not be too long, especially if there be small children in the family. A few verses of scripture, or a short psalm is often better than a long chapter. It is best to have some plan of Bible reading, either by books or by topics.

2. The prayer, too, should not only be brief, but very simple in its language, and very practical in its requests. If John or Mary be sick, pray for them by name.

3. Let the worship be characterized by cheerful reverence. Gloom, or moroseness, will make it distasteful to the young. Do not go about it as a task to be dreaded, but as a blessed privilege to be enjoyed.

4. If possible, the worship should embrace a familiar song. The children will enjoy this.

5. In the reading of scriptures, it would be well frequently, if not always, to have all the family read, either in turn or responsively.

6. Where there is time for it, a brief word of comment or of explanation to the children, would be well. It should be permitted to any member of the family to ask any question in reference to the lesson read.

7. If neither parent, nor any member of the family feels able to pray in the presence of the others, at first, let one of the following prayers be read aloud, while all devoutly join in the sentiments expressed. Or, let the Lord's Prayer be recited together, the family bowing. In a little while, of course, there would be no need of depending on these forms.

8. The character of the worship; especially of the prayer, should be determined by the surroundings or condition of the family. But be sure to let thanksgiving have a place in every prayer.

9. Above all, seek to make the very atmosphere of your

home life, that of religious cheerfulness. Let your children see that religion is not melancholy, and that family worship is not inconsistent with a game of "blind man's buff," or any other innocent amusement; but that it is inconsistent with selfishness, peevishness, bad temper, shirking of duty, falsehood, deceit, and impurity in thought, word, or deed.

MORNING PRAYERS

1. Lord's Day Morning

Father of lights, who wakens the eyes of man to look upon the dayspring that makes all things new, we praise you for your care over us through the silent watches of the night, and hail with thanksgiving the freshness of the morning.

O you, by whose mercy we have all been spared, through the week that is past, your children draw nigh to worship you with gladness on the morning of our Savior's resurrection. It is the day that you have made; assist us to rejoice in it and be glad.

Be pleased, O Lord, to bless this day, the preaching of the Word of your grace. Anoint the lips of your ministers. Open the ears of all who hear, and turn their hearts to you. Over the whole earth let the gospel of mercy run and have free course. Set at liberty the slaves of sin. Let the feet of such as go astray in error or in doubt be turned into the way of truth. Let careless souls be aroused and the hard heart be melted. For every sower of the seed of life, we beg your blessing, which gives increase. Animate and direct in their sacred office all pastors, missionaries, and Sunday-school teachers. Lend to every one who speaks for Jesus, courage and ardor, wisdom and hopefulness; that the glory of his cross may be spread abroad in every place.

Consider, we entreat you, the wants of such as through sickness or domestic duty are withheld from public worship. Grant them access to your throne of mercy, and may your Spirit be their guest.

Assuage the anxiety of those who watch beside the sick or dying. Help all who nurse little children to bear with them in gentleness. Comfort the bed-ridden and the aged. Forsake not your servants who are old and gray-haired, but cheer their failing hearts with the prospect of a brighter home. Enable all who are called, in the needful service of others, to sacrifice a portion of their day of rest, to do it cheerfully in the spirit of love; and do you yourself compensate them for the sacrifice by the rich treasures of your grace.

The Lord be pleased to listen to the voice of these our supplications. The Lord cause all labor which is done for Christ our King to be our delight, and all rest to be wearisome which is not rest in him. The Lord grant that what things are pleasing unto him we may ardently desire and fully attain. The Lord lift up the light of his countenance upon us all this day, and bless his whole Church with peace. Through the Name of your only Son, Jesus Christ, our Savior. Amen!

2. Lord's Day Morning

We bless you with lowly hearts, O Lord, because you have spared us to enter once more upon your day of rest where you pour out blessings abundantly upon your children. Give us, we entreat you, a larger measure of the Holy Spirit. Visit and revive our weary spirits. Grant us a godly sorrow for sin, wholesome knowledge of our own defects, and hearty desire after spiritual benefits. Admit us this day, with all your Christian worshipers, to the bliss of forgiveness and the fellowship of the saints. Reveal to us, as to your whole Church, the glory of your love in the face of Jesus Christ. May this day of privilege assist each one of us to live the new life of faith in the Son of God and of obedience to your holy will. Refresh us with your grace, and bring forth in us all the sweet and profitable fruits of good living, through the indwelling of your Holy Spirit.

Let your word, O Father, which you have given for the healing of the nations, be published far and near this day. Touch with fire the lips of your messengers. Open to your message the hearts of those that hear. Draw the wistful, the wandering, and the weary within your fold. Comfort all penitents with the assurance of pardon. Sprinkle the guilty who confess their faults with the blood of cleansing. Carry in your bosom, safe from harm, the young and tender.

Grant that they may constantly escape the rough trials of life and the malice of their spiritual foe. Bless for them today the lesson of the church, of the home, and of the school, that, being nurtured in your doctrine, they may be trained for your service.

Let the sick, and such as by reason of needful duty at home cannot attend your house of prayer, be mercifully assisted to raise their affections unto yourself, while in private they wait upon your blessing. Deny them not the welcome refreshment of your Word. Withhold not from them the helpful influence of your Spirit. But upon them and upon us all, and upon your church universal, redeemed unto your praise, be grace, mercy, and peace, for Jesus' sake. Amen!

3. Lord's Day Morning

It is good for us, O Lord, that you have cast this island in the stream, and built the Lord's day all around where we stand and are secure. No sound of secular occupation disturbs us; we are at rest. And we lift up our thoughts unto themes which the week disallows, and have leisure of meditation, and can draw very near to you and abide under the shadow of your wing. Now we are no longer chafed and fretted by care; no longer heated by rivalries one with another; we can look out, as from a window, and see the storm of worldly things out of which we have come, and pass judgment upon them, and measure again our thoughts and our joys—yea, search into the deep places of our heart and know our own selves before you.

You, O God, can quiet the quaking heart as easily as you do the storm and the rushing of the waves. We ask you to take to yourself today the unquiet, the disturbed, those that suffer in mind, and speak those words of consolation to them which they need; for you know who suffer from long depression, who suffer from the vexatious burdens of secular things; you know who seem to themselves, unfortunate in life, cast out, neglected; those whose purposes are crossed, and whose very aims and ends of life seem to them subverted. You can make them feel that they are dear to you, and that they possess you, that in you they have all joy and all wealth. We ask you that you will draw near to those that are in trouble, that they may not be alarmed by it, nor think that any strange thing have surprised them.

May they behold themselves initiated by their sorrow into the true brotherhood of the great human family; may they perceive that they are united to Christ, the Head of humanity and the Captain of our salvation, made perfect through suffering; and may they rejoice to have suffering, if through its ministration they may learn more and more of faith, of patience, of hope, of submission, and of love.

We pray that you will deliver us from worldly-mindedness. Keep us from growing sordid under those duties that we must needs perform. May we watch our thoughts, lest we should grow selfish by prosperity. May we walk humbly before God, and not fail to recognize that spiritual connection between your blessing and our success; and so may we desire every day to go back from all our outgoings, all our blossomings, and fruit-bearings, to you that are the root from which we spring.

O Lord God, we pray that you will bless the young in this household. We pray also for other households; may we love each other's children; may we have sympathy in the care and burden of their rearing, and help each other. We ask you that our children may not forget what love their parents have for them; and, as they grow up to years of discretion, may they enter into the blessedness and treasure of Christian knowledge and of Christian life.

Grant that we may be held back from all malign and passionate influences, that we may be conscientious and earnest, yet full of love. May we forget no truths in our zeal for any truth; may we understand the whole will of God, and be kept in the very spirit of Christ, and do our Master's work in our Master's spirit. For Christ's sake. Amen!

4. Monday Morning

O Lord, who is good and ready to forgive, and plenteous in mercy unto all that call upon you, we thank you that our days are not passed away in your wrath. We are not consumed by your anger, but are made glad by your love. You are gracious to us and full of compassion, our refuge in time of trouble, our strength and our song.

Help us to remember through this week the vows that we uttered yesterday, and the resolutions that we formed to obey your commandments. Suffer us not to be carried away from you by the returning tide of our common life. May the vision of your glory remain with us, undimmed by the mists and clouds of unbelief and sin. Do you in your great mercy remember our prayers even when we forget them. Leave us not to ourselves: our trust is in you.

If any sorrow should fall upon us, let not our faith in your goodness be shaken. If we require chastisement for our own sins, may we remember that whom the Lord loves he chastens; and if we suffer through the sins of others, may we take it patiently, knowing that you have laid on Christ the sins of us all.

Watch over those whom we love, and keep them in your ways. Be with them on sea or on land; and whether they be near to us or far away, may they all dwell in you.

Bless all Christian people, and may they all live under the constant control of your great love for them, and may they be saved from the perils that beset them in this world by their hope of eternal glory. Hear us, O Lord, and have mercy upon us for Christ's sake. Amen!

5. Monday Morning

O God, you are our God; early will we seek you. Because your lovingkindness is better than life, therefore our lips shall praise you.

We bless you that you have been about us by night as a shade upon our right hand, so that, spared by your providence, our eyes awake to greet the new day. We thank you for strength restored through sleep, and for the spiritual refreshment we yesterday enjoyed as we thought of your lovingkindness in the midst of your temple.

Now, Lord, that we enter upon our everyday duties, assist us to perform our vows. Our desire is to devote every hour of the day and every talent we possess to the service of him who purchased us with his own blood. We are not our own. Yours we are, and you would we serve. Suffer no gift of yours to lie unused, or to be misspent in the service of sin. May we bring forth fruit unto holiness, that the end may be life everlasting.

Defend us, great Captain of our salvation, against the errors that mislead us, and the foes that waylay our steps as Christian pilgrims. Give us a clear eye to see the path of duty, and confidence to know that it will prove the path of safety. May self-interest never tempt us aside from what integrity requires; nor the dread of consequences make our hand falter in doing what is right. Grant us a brave, patient, and hopeful temper; that whatever trouble may befall, we may seek before everything else the kingdom of God and his righteousness.

O God, we beg of you an open hand and a generous heart. Keep our ears from hearing scandal, and our tongue from bearing tales. Cause us to delight in the prosperity of our fellows, and in their adversity to succor them cheerfully. For ourselves we ask neither poverty nor riches, but that you would choose our inheritance for us, and teach us to meet all changes of fortune with a placid mind. Should you darken our home with loss or fear of change, Lord, help us to resign with submission what we have enjoyed with temperance. Spare to us one another's love, we humbly pray you. Let life and health be prolonged; but if your wisdom see good to afflict us, hold us back from murmuring, and instruct us how to say, "Your will be done."

These, and all other needful mercies, we beg for the sake of your only-begotten Son, our Savior Jesus Christ. Amen!

6. Monday Morning

O Lord, we thank you for the tender care with which you have watched over us during the hours of sleep, and for the comfort and health in which we arise this morning. Help us to carry into the busy hours of the week all the holy impressions and resolutions of your day. Grant us grace to pursue our secular calling in a Christian spirit. May our most trivial occupations be ennobled by the principles of the gospel of Christ; may all our works be sanctified by the Word of God and prayer. May we honor you by the uprightness and integrity of our conduct, by the unselfishness and generosity of our spirit, and by our endeavor in all things to obey the law of Christ. May we not covet the wealth of this world, but desire to employ whatever we gain for the good of those who are dear to us, and for the service of our Lord. While not slothful in business, may we be fervent in spirit, serving the Lord. Whatever we eat or drink, or whatever we do, may we do all for the glory of God.

And, Father, we pray that in our home life we may act worthily of you. May we be ever conscious of the presence of our Lord, and seek to manifest his spirit. May we be gentle and forbearing toward each other, and faithful in rendering toward all in the household their respective dues. May we minister to one another's welfare, and guard against selfishness in thought and word and deed. Save us from luxury and display, from pride and vainglory, from the snares of ambition and the desire of human applause, and help us to walk humbly with our God.

May those who are young, especially, learn to value everything according to its tendency to make them just and pure and good. May they become truly wise through the teaching of your Holy Spirit.

At all times we are exposed to temptation, and in the excitement and absorption of business we are liable to forget our danger. Let us not be off our guard this day. Allow us to run into no sin, but keep us in all our ways. May we be in the fear of the Lord all the day long, and may the remembrance of your presence be our strength.

O most merciful Father, we pray you to forgive all our sins, and to preserve us by your mighty power through faith unto salvation. We pray for all blessings through Jesus Christ our Lord. Amen!

7. Other Mornings

O God, our Heavenly Father, by whose love all creatures are made blessed, we give thanks for all that makes you known to us, and bless your name for every gift of yours; for our parents and teachers, companions and friends; for our homes and our work, and all that makes us happy. We bless you for your tender care; for your eye upon us by day and by night; for your Holy Spirit in our hearts; for your correction when we err, and your forgiveness when we repent; and for the Savior who turns us from evil ways to your holy and blessed service. We pray you for a pure heart and a right spirit, that we may do that which is pleasing unto you. Make us careful not to offend in thought, or word, or deed. May we speak the truth always and love it forever. As we grow in years may we grow in wisdom, and in favor with God and man. When we sin, do you forgive us; when we repent, do you restore us. When we wander, bring us back; and when we are careless, O Lord, do you correct us. Breathe into our souls, O heavenly Father, the love of whatsoever is true, and beautiful, and good. May we fear to be unfaithful, and have no other fear. Forgive us all our sins, and keep us from sinning again. Help us to remember that we are your children, and belong to you. Enable us to love others as you have loved us. Make us generous and kind to all, faithful in duty, truthful in speech, and sweet in temper. Enlighten our minds that we may know you, inspire our hearts that we may love you, and guide our wills that we may serve you forever.

Make us children of the light of the day; upright, simple, free from guile. Make us faithful and cheerful, just and kind to all. May we help and not hinder each other in the knowledge of you, and in the doing of your will. Bless our neighbors and friends with the like gift of the heavenly grace, and so direct our paths and inspire our lives that we may all at last inherit that kingdom which you have prepared for them that love you; through Jesus Christ our Lord. Amen!

8. Other Mornings

Almighty God, we bless you for the rest of another night, and that we awake this day in life, and in so much health and enjoyment. We ask you to shine upon us, and teach us how to spend the coming day. May all we do be done honestly and faithfully. Preserve and deepen our trust in you and your providence. Increase our confidence in your love, wisdom, and justice; that so we may not live without God in the world. Whatsoever our hands find to do may we do it with our might. May we begin our labor modestly and continue it in self-forgetfulness. Deliver us from all weakness and fearfulness from want of purpose or misgiving. Grant us simplicity and earnestness in our ways; and whether we succeed in our purposes or fail, may we be upright in heart before you. Preserve us this day from all sloth and idleness, and from the misuse of what you have entrusted to our care; and forasmuch as the business of this life is apt to steal our hearts from you, give us grace to remember that we have a Master in heaven, and to live as seeing him who is invisible.

In our temptations guard us, and in all difficulty uphold us. You have taught us not to think of ourselves only, but also of the wants of others, and we remember before you all who are burdened and oppressed; those whose hopes have been crushed, and whose purposes are overthrown. We remember all who are afflicted by poverty, or worn down by illness; the weary and heavy laden; those who are enduring wrong, or suffering for righteousness' sake; those also who are in darkness or despair. And we commend unto you, O you Father of our spirits, those who are about to depart this life, beseeching you to grant unto them the spirit of tranquillity and trustfulness. May they put their hope in you; and, having passed through the valley of the shadow of death, may they enter into the rest that remains for the people of God.

Help us, O God, to spend this day, as if it were our last on earth, in willing obedience to your Holy Will and when the end of our earthly pilgrimage shall have been reached, receive us all into our heavenly home, through riches of grace in Christ Jesus our Lord. Amen!

9. Other Mornings

O Lord God, you are our refuge and our hope; in you alone we rest: for we find all to be weak and insufficient but you. Many friends cannot profit, nor strong helpers assist, nor prudent counselors advise, nor the books of the learned afford comfort, nor any precious substance deliver, nor any place give shelter, unless you yourself do assist, strengthen, console, instruct and guard us.

To you, therefore, do we lift up our eyes; in you, our God, the Father of mercies, do we put our trust. Bless and sanctify our souls, that they may become thy holy habitation, and the seat of your eternal glory; and let nothing be found in us displeasing in your sight. Protect us and keep us amidst all dangers; and, accompanying us by your grace, direct us along the way of peace to your everlasting home, where, with all the redeemed and sanctified, we shall praise you forever through Jesus Christ our Redeemer. Amen!

10. Other Mornings

O Lord Almighty, who is merciful and gracious, long-suffering and of great goodness, we approach you as the God of mercy, imploring you to hear these our prayers, and to pardon the multitude of our sins, for the sake of Jesus Christ. Day after day we add to the number of our transgressions; every night we have the sins of the preceding day to repent of; and every morning we have reason to fear lest we should again yield to temptation, and return to our former iniquities. O Lord, put your Spirit into all our hearts; that we, being made pure and holy in our secret thoughts, may not fail to perform all that is good and acceptable in your sight.

Dispose each of us on this day habitually to employ our several faculties in your service. While we pursue the various duties of our calling, may we have a single eye to your glory; and may we undertake no employment on which we cannot hope for your blessing. May no spirit of self-indulgence, no love of ease, no dread of opposition, no fear of shame, prevent our laying out our lives heartily in your service. Make us willing to deny ourselves, that we may live unto you. Teach us to enter into the spirit of those Christians and Apostles of old, who counted not their lives dear unto themselves, so that they might finish their course with joy. Grant unto every member of this family your peace, and all your heavenly consolations; and make us to be of one heart and of one mind, praising you for your mercies, praying to you for your grace, and uniting in the confession of our daily sins before you.

Establish us in your faith, and fear, and love; and enlighten us, that we may understand your whole will concerning us. Where we mistake, have pity on our errors; and if we have wandered from the right way, do you in mercy bring us back. Lead us, O Lord, into the paths of righteousness and peace. May we watch our hearts, and bridle our tongues, and govern our tempers. May we be ready to forgive, even as we hope to be forgiven. May we be steadfast and immovable, always abounding in the work of the Lord, knowing that our labor shall not be in vain in the Lord.

We now commit ourselves to you for this day; help us to live according to these our prayers ; and thus may we be prepared for your heavenly kingdom; we ask it for our Savior's sake. Amen!

11. Other Mornings

We bless you, our Father in heaven, that you have kept us through another night, in which you have given rest and sleep.

We rejoice that you have brought us to behold the light of another day, with its duties and privileges. We thank you that our lives have been precious in your sight. And now we pray your guidance throughout this day to which your mercy has brought us. Give us today our daily bread. Forgive our sins. Help us to forgive those who wrong us. We invoke your blessing in its fullness upon our loved ones, whether they kneel with us here this morning, or are far from us. You are near to all. Keep, O God, from sickness, from danger, and from sin. May the consciousness of your love go with us, and your presence guide us through this day. We ask not that we may walk in our own way, but in your way. Help us to do your will this day. May we labor to be accepted in the Beloved, whose we are and whom we serve. For Jesus sake. Amen!

EVENING PRAYERS

1. Lord's Day Evening

Father and almighty God, whom truly to know is eternal life: give us grace to approach you this evening with penitent and believing hearts, and to enjoy communion with you, by your Holy Spirit, through Jesus Christ our Lord.

We thank you, O God, for the opportunities which have been this day given us, of worshipping you and communing with you in your house of prayer. It is of your mercy alone that you have borne with us all these years, have not cast us away for our ingratitude, nor cut us off in our wickedness. Grant that our hearts may be so touched by the remembrance of your long patience and forbearance toward us, that we may give ourselves up to you in loving devotion, and walk before you in true holiness all the remaining days of our life.

Forgive, O Father, for Jesus Christ's sake, all the coldness and indifference, all the wandering of thought and imagination, which you have seen in our worship, in public and in private, this day. Quicken our interest in holy and heavenly things. Give us a living faith in the Word of your revelation, and grace both to love what you command and to desire that which you do promise.

Bless with us, O Lord, all who are dear to us, our relatives, friends and neighbors. Bless the congregation in which we worship, and those who minister to us in holy things. Unite all who name the name of Christ in one hope and faith and love. May they be one flock under One Shepherd, Jesus Christ, Our Lord, to whom with the Father, and the Holy Spirit, be all glory and praise forever and ever. Amen!

2. Lord's Day Evening

O God, our heavenly Father, in you the whole family of your saints rests and is glad. Let your blessing abide on all who have worshipped with us today, on all for whom we have prayed, and on all who have been praying for us. Give the earth peace, O God, and crown the year with increase. Fill our land with piety, virtue, and contentment. Rule, in your fear, the hearts of those who are our rulers. Be pleased to guide the young in your ways of pleasantness. Let the parched places of your church be revived with grace. Widen the boundaries of your kingdom. Clothe with power and with salvation the ministers of your Word, and cause the ends of the earth to see the salvation of our God.

God of the night as of the day, who has drawn around your weary world the curtain of darkness, let all your children sleep secure.

Give pure and blameless slumber to every inmate of our dwelling, with restoration of vigor to serve you through the working days that follow. As Lord's days come and go, may each one bring us nearer to our home, and leave us fitter for it; till, purified and trained through the discipline of our present state, you bid us exchange these brief intervals of rest below for the endless worship and sinless fellowship of our Father's house above.

Grant this, O God, for the honor of our Advocate and Mediator, Jesus Christ. Amen

3. Lord's Day Evening

O God, whose home on high has perfect rest, your children bless you for the stillness and the hush of this one day, whereby you do break for them the care and toil of the working week. We thank you for a pause in labor; for seasons of sacred praise; for the refreshing of the heart through the intercourse of our home; for your house, for the Word of truth, and for all the sacred and hallowed influences of the day. Let your strength and your peace abide with us, we ask you. We shall have need of both; for tomorrow will bring back the duties that exhaust, and the anxieties that fret us. Oh, let the memory of what we have experienced soothe us through the week. Make us the fitter to serve, as seeing you beside us, feeling you to be very near. Breathe over all our common work the temper of our worship, and encourage us to sustain the better our earthly load by the hope of your heavenly rest that remains for those who love you.

We commend to you the suffering, the solitary, and the bereaved. Show yourself pitiful unto any among our friends or neighbors, whose need, by reason of sickness or other trial, we know to be exceeding great. Guard such as journey by sea or land. Assist the aged to compose themselves for their departure. Be a protector to tempted innocence, and restrain the violence of power. Gently reconcile the mourner to his loss, and teach the widow's heart to lean upon yourself.

O you who slumbers not, be pleased to bestow upon all our household refreshing sleep. Lighten our darkness, we ask you. Defend us against all perils of this night. Keep us in holy concord. Grant us pure affections, sound health and cheerful tempers. Implant within our children your godly fear; and so train them to the paths of wisdom and obedience, that unto their lives' end they may walk before you in holiness and righteousness.

Finally, O Father, we pray you to sanctify us, each one, through the changes and discipline of this mortal life, to the end that we miss not that everlasting repose, which you have promised to your saints; but, through the unspeakable merit of our Redeemer's passion, (to whom be endless praise!) may we, and all whom we love, be counted worthy to inherit the glory to be revealed, the inheritance incorruptible, undefiled, and that fades not away. Amen!

4. Other Evenings

Again, O God, we come to render you thanks for the mercies of another day and to implore your care and blessing for the night. Give, Eternal Father, rest to our weariness; when we are weak and restless, renew our strength.

O you, who neither slumbers nor sleeps, lighten our eyes with your light, that we sleep not in death.

Keep us from all terror by night, and from the pestilence that walks in darkness, as from the destruction at noonday.

Give us rest, as from toil, so from every evil thought; and visit us with visions of wisdom, or with quiet of refreshment.

From all illusion of fond fancy or terror, from evil remembrance, and evil designing, keep us, dear Lord.

You in whose book all our members are written, grant us wholesome rest, free from terror and burden, with holy trust and peace.

You are our Maker and our Judge, but also our Father, Savior, and Friend; deny not the comfort of your Holy Spirit to your children.

Shelter our slumber with the wing of your pity; let our awakening be in good time, a time of blessing and of prayer.

Early in the morning will we seek you, with thanksgiving and zeal for your service.

Into your hands, O Lord, we commend ourselves, our spirits, souls, and bodies, to our Maker, Preserver, Life-giver.

Bless with us every friend, benefactor, and connection, whom you have granted to us in goodness, and bound us to with duty.

Guard our lying down, and our rising up, henceforth, Lord, and forever.

Let us remember you in resting, and when we wake up, be present with you.

We will lay us down in peace, and take our rest; for you, O Father, only make us dwell in safety. For our Savior's sake. Amen!

5. Other Evenings

Lord, we beg most humbly that the service that we have this day offered unto you may find acceptance in your eyes. Nourished by your bounty, made joyful in your gifts, we desire to spend our time to your praise. The transgressions of this day lay not to our charge, we entreat you. But grant that, at peace with you and with all men, we may lay our tired bodies to the night's repose in childlike reliance upon your protection. Shepherd of Israel, give your angels charge over your people, that as you have kept them in their ways by day, so they may be guarded through their rest by night.

Visit with your divine charity the helpless, the sick, and the forlorn. May the slumber of infants be light and calm. Let not pain disturb the pillow of our little ones, nor any harm threaten our dwelling. Be near our distant dear ones and shield them from every alarm. Let happy thoughts of you engage the wakeful hours of the aged; but banish vexing regret from the memory of the mourner.

Finally, we commend one another to the tender keeping of the Heavenly Father, and to the comfortable fellowship of the Holy Spirit, and to the sympathy of the ever-blessed Son, our Brother and our Advocate: unto whom be, glory on earth as it is in heaven. Amen!

6. Other Evenings

Almighty and most merciful Father, we would come before you this night, confessing our sins. Another day is gone to its account; and we know and feel, O Lord, in how many things it must witness against us. We have left undone those things that we ought to have done, and we have done those things that we ought not to have done. We have been often careless and worldly, selfish and indifferent; we have neglected opportunities of doing good both by word and action. We have not served you this day, nor loved you as we ought to have done. Forgive us, for our Lord Jesus Christ's sake, all that is past. Give us grace, before we rest this night, to devote ourselves entirely to you, that we may be yours in body and soul, and walk before you in love till we come to be with you forever.

Bless with us, O Heavenly Father, all whom we love and who love us; all to whom we are indebted for any help or comfort in our lives; all who are under our charge, authority or influence.

Accept, O God, our praises and thanksgivings for all your mercies bestowed upon us. For life and health, for food and clothing, and for all the comforts of our home; for every faculty and opportunity for kindness and affection and brotherly love; for our knowledge of you as our Father and of Jesus Christ as our Savior, and of the Holy Spirit as our Comforter; for the means of grace and communion with you, and for the hope which you have given us of a place hereafter in your presence. We ask you to fill us with your love and heavenly benediction, through Jesus Christ, our only Mediator and Redeemer. Amen!

7. Other Evenings

Blessed Lord, we are gathered again before you, to ask your blessing upon the hours of darkness, and to thank you for the mercies of the past day. Pour upon us the spirit of grace and supplication, that no wandering or irreverent thoughts may mingle with this offering of our evening sacrifice, through Jesus Christ our Lord.

Take this house and every inmate of it, under your gracious protection this night. May we lie down at peace with you, through our Lord Jesus Christ; may we rest in your charge, who slumbers not nor sleeps, and awake to be with you all the day long.

Look in mercy, O Lord, upon the earth which you have made, and upon all the sorrows and miseries of your creatures. We would commend especially to your Fatherly compassion all who mourn for sin; all upon whom the hand of punishment and judgment lies heavily, and who have not yet found forgiveness and cleansing in the blood and in the spirit of Jesus Christ. Lift up the light of your countenance upon them, O Lord, who would not that any should perish, but that all should come to repentance.

Bless your church universal, and make it the joy and the blessing of the whole earth. Grant that all who profess and call themselves Christians may walk according to the Word and the example of their Lord and Master.

O heavenly Father, make us, and all who are dear to us, true and living members of the body of Jesus Christ; that, living here in the light of your truth, we may attain at last to the light of everlasting life, and dwell forever in your heavenly presence, through our Lord Jesus Christ; to whom, with you and the Holy Spirit, be all honor and glory, world without end. Amen!

8. Other Evenings

Almighty God, Creator of heaven and earth, who from the beginning did appoint the day and the night to succeed each other, and have, now by your providence brought us once again through the hours of toil to the time of resting; be with us, we pray you, during the season of darkness, and cause the light of your countenance to shine upon our souls.

O God, we cannot tell how often we have offended you this day; you alone search the heart, and see us as we are. Show us, we pray you, that which is amiss in us, that by your grace we may truly repent and strive earnestly to amend our lives. Forgive all that is past, for the sake of our Lord Jesus Christ, who died for the sins of the world.

Let your Fatherly hand be over us through this night, and through the days that may be yet to come. Give us grace to be ever waiting and watching for the coming of our Lord Jesus Christ.

Bless our country. Give wisdom to those who rule; and to all who are under authority a spirit of docility and obedience. May we be a nation fearing you and working righteousness.

Finally, we pray for one another, and for all those who are dear to any of us. Unite us as one household in the bonds of Christian love. May our hearts be set to please you in all things and to advance that kingdom which is peace and righteousness and joy. O you of whom every family in heaven and earth is named, be the Father, we pray you, of this household, and let your peace and your blessing rest upon it day and night, till we all come, in your mercy and goodness, to that heavenly home whence we shall go out no more forever.

Grant this, we humbly ask you, for the sake of your Son Jesus Christ, our only Mediator and Redeemer. Amen!

9. Saturday Evening

We thank you O Lord, for the wonderful goodness of your providence during another day and another week. Still we are preserved by your kind and effectual care. Our health continues, our home comforts are perpetuated by you. We meet together tonight and close the week once more in peace. The shadow of no great trouble has fallen on us. Thanks forever be unto your blessed name; and may the love which has followed us through all the scenes of the day, and all the circumstances of the week, be with us through the watches of this night. May we lie down under your protection, sleep through your gift of rest, and wake refreshed by that slumber which is your gift and will prepare us for the holy engagements of the coming Lord's day. May earthly cares and troubles be forgotten by us, except so far as they may stimulate our devotion, and furnish subject for prayer and holy meditation. All we ask is in the name of our Lord Jesus Christ, to whom, with you and the Holy Spirit, be everlasting praises. Amen!

10. Saturday Evening

Most holy and most merciful God, we give you thanks that you have brought us in safety through all the perils of another week. And whether you have led us through green pastures and beside still waters, or along rough and rocky paths, we bless you that you have not forsaken us, nor have you suffered us to wander altogether beyond the hearing of your voice or the reach of your protecting hand. We began the week with you, and with you we close it.

Now that the day of rest and fellowship with yourself is near, help us to escape from all that has irritated, vexed, and excited us as the week has been passing by. Give us your peace. May we cast our care upon you, that we may be at liberty to rejoice in the vision of your face, and to worship you with reverence and devout fear. Let not the transient disappointments or the transient triumphs of our common life be permitted to come between our hearts and yourself.

We entreat you to let your Spirit rest on all those with whom we shall meet for worship. Prepare them for the great duty and the great blessedness to which they will be called. Tonight, before they sleep, may such thoughts of yourself come to them as shall make them earnestly long to see your glory. If any of them have never yet repented of their sin, reveal to them their sad estate, their guilt, and their peril, and grant them true repentance.

Let all the Christian work which shall be done tomorrow be done devoutly and zealously, wisely and hopefully; and may many who shall lie down tonight with their sins unforgiven and their hearts unrenewed, obtain forgiveness and eternal life before the coming day of rest shall close. May the world be nearer to you tomorrow night than it is now. Grant your good Spirit to your servant from whom we shall receive instruction in Christian truth and duty. May we be conscious that the words that we hear from his lips came first from you.

Have us in your strong and merciful keeping tonight. Forgive all the sins we have committed during the week. Forgive the sins of all whom we love. For Christ's sake. Amen!

11. Saturday Evening

Our Father, who is in heaven, at the close of another week we, your children, unite in offering to you our tributes of praise and thanksgiving. Receive, we ask you, the homage of our spirits tonight, the offering of our entire being to yourself, and help us more and more to love you with all our hearts.

We thank you for the blessings of the week now closing. Life, time, reason, domestic and social happiness, protection from danger, deliverance from the power of the wicked one, and all the supplies of temporal and spiritual mercies have come to us from you. You opened your hand and satisfied our desires, yea, have abundantly exceeded all we could have asked or thought. O Lord, help us to praise you. Preserve us from insensibility, from hardness of heart, from receiving your mercies as necessary or common things. In each one we should see your hand; on each should behold your image and superscription; while we should remember that all come to us through Christ, and for the sake of his wonderful life and death.

We pray you to forgive the sins of the week. Our hearts condemn us for many thoughts, feelings, words, acts, which have been unholy, and displeasing to you. Enter not into judgment with us, O Lord. We present ourselves before you in the name of Jesus; by renewed faith we appropriate to ourselves the perfect righteousness of your Son; and we pray that for his sake our consciences may be cleansed, calmed, and purified, and our sins forgiven.

Prepare us now for rest and the service of the Lord's day. Even on this its threshold, in this its outer court, we would feel its sacred influence. We bless you for your holy day. After the night's rest may it rise upon us calmly and brightly, whispering to us of your love and inviting us to your worship. Thus as our weeks pass, and Lord's days come and go, may we, and all we love, be prepared for higher service, and nobler worship in the world of light and bliss. We thank you that there remains a rest for the people of God. By faith we would now enter into it, and by hope anticipate its future and perfect enjoyment. Teach and help us to live worthy of it, and at last permit us to form an unbroken circle in heaven; for the Redeemer's sake. Amen!

THANKS BEFORE MEALS

We give you thanks, Our Father, for these bounties of your providence, and pray you to sanctify them to the nourishment of our bodies, and to feed our spirits with your truth and grace; in Jesus Christ, our Lord. Amen!

For these temporal gifts, and for all other mercies from your loving hand, accept, O Father, our grateful thanks; in Christ's name. Amen

In these blessings now before us, we see the tokens of your loving care, most gracious Father, and tender you grateful acknowledgments; in Jesus' name. Amen!

Lord God, heavenly Father, bless unto us these your gifts, which of your tender kindness you have bestowed upon us; through Jesus Christ our Lord. Amen!

Almighty God, heavenly Father, we give you thanks for all your gifts and goodness; and pray you, as you feed our bodies, so also graciously keep our souls in the true faith and confession of your name; through Jesus Christ our Lord. Amen!

We give you thanks, O God our Father, for all your benefits, through Jesus Christ our Lord, who, with you, lives and reigns world without end. Amen!

Our heavenly Father, sanctify to our use, we ask you, these provisions of your love, and us to yourself and your service. Amen!

We accept, O Lord, these gifts as from you, who are the giver of every good and perfect gift that descends from above. Teach us, in receiving them, as we live upon your bounty so to live for your glory; for Christ's sake. Amen!

We praise you, O Father, for our daily bread, and all the blessings of your good providence. While we feed thus upon your bounty may we spend our strength in doing good; in Jesus' name. Amen!

Accept of our gratitude, O Lord, for this social and Christian fellowship, and for all the bounties of your providence and your grace; through Jesus Christ our Lord. Amen!

O Lord, we greatly thank you, for life and all its blessings. We give you thanks for the health and comforts of the morning, and for these means of life and health. We pray you, O Father, hear our prayer for the continuance of these favors, and accept of our thanksgiving; through Jesus Christ our Lord. Amen!

Father, we thank you, that we have laid us down and slept and awaked; for you, God, have preserved us. We thank you for food and raiment. Give us each day our daily bread. Bless us to your work, and bless all your workers; in the name of Christ our Redeemer. Amen!

FOR SPECIAL EVENTS AND SEASONS

On a Member of the Family Leaving Home

Almighty God, our Heavenly Father, of whom every family in heaven and earth is named, we bow once more before you as a united family. How gracious you have been to us in all these years! We thank you for all you have made us to each other, for the love that binds us together. You have made us to dwell together in peace and unity, under this family roof-tree, and to share each other's joys and sorrows. And now, O Lord, our circle is about to be broken. We ask your blessing upon him [or her] who now goes out from us. Shield him from danger of every kind. O do you strengthen him by your grace that he may overcome the temptations that will beset his path. May he never forget you, nor his parents, nor any of the loved ones at the old home, nor the training he has here received. May he ever seek to honor the God of his father and of his mother, no matter what may be his surroundings or employment. May the enticements of the wicked one never allure him from the straight and narrow way that leads unto life. If he be led into sin, O do you grant him the grace of repentance, that he may seek your forgiveness, and renewed strength. Whether it ever be our lot in life to bow together again around the same family altar, grant, we ask you, that we all may meet in your many-mansioned house, in heaven, to praise you eternally and go out no more forever. For Christ's sake. Amen!

For Our Children

Almighty God, our ever-gracious Heavenly Father; among the gifts of your loving providence, for which we do humbly thank you, are the children whom you have given us. But O, do you strengthen us for the duty you have laid upon us of training them up for you. May we be careful to provide, not only for their bodies and their minds, but especially for their moral and spiritual culture. Forbid that we should train them only in the knowledge of this world and leave them in ignorance of your will and their obligations to obey it. Grant that we may realize that their present and future happiness and usefulness depend far more on their religious training, than on any uncertain riches or other material advantages we may bestow upon them. Give us patience and self-control, that we provoke them not to wrath, and help us, both by the example of our daily lives and by precept, to bring them up in the nurture and admonition of the Lord. May we not spoil them by over indulgence, on the one hand, nor embitter their lives by unreasonable exactions on the other. As you have drawn us to you by love, so may we be enabled, by divine help, to bind our children to us, to our home and to you, by cords of love. Save, O Lord, save our precious children from the snares of the wicked one, and in our Father's house may we all praise you at last, a united family, forever, through the grace of our Lord Jesus Christ, to whom with the Father and the Holy Spirit be glory evermore. Amen!

On a Bright Day in Summer

O you who make the glorious sun go forth as a bridegroom out of his chamber, and rejoice as a giant to run his course, so that nothing is hid from the heat thereof: we bless you for the light of this world; for the joy of beholding the day; for the fruits and flowers with which you in your bounty have decked the earth. We bless you for the garden and the field; for the basket and the store.

And yet, O Lord, what were these without yourself? What were the light of the sun, if our souls were in the shadow of death and the night of ignorance? May the Sun of Righteousness, even the Lord Jesus Christ, never cease to shine within us. May the kindly warmth of your Holy Spirit penetrate our hearts with heavenly love. And so may our earthly be changed into your heavenly: and the desert of our nature rejoice and blossom as the rose. And may we, receiving evermore the good seed of your word, bring forth the fruit of righteousness to your praise and glory; through Jesus Christ our Lord. Amen!

Christmas Day

Almighty God, who have given your only-begotten Son to take our nature upon him, and to be born of a pure virgin: Grant that we being regenerate, and made your children by adoption and grace, may daily be renewed by your Holy Spirit. May this glad and happy season be used by us for spiritual culture, and not marred by unseemly revelry. May there come to our souls a deeper sense of your infinite love and grace; through the name of our Lord Jesus Christ, who lives and reigns with you and the Holy Spirit, ever one God, world without end. Amen!

New Year's Day

Grant, O God, now that we have entered on another year, that, for the sake of the truth, and for the sake of holiness, we may be lifted up to a higher life. May we endeavor to take a clearer and a truer conception of duty. May we, for Christ's sake, and for the sake of his cause, consecrate ourselves afresh to you. You, O God, can lift us up; and only you can do it. All our courage will be in vain, and all our good resolutions will sleep as sentinels over-wearied at their post, and we shall be surprised and destroyed, if you are not vigilant for us, and your grace is not exercised in our behalf. We stand begging, not because you need to be begged, and are reluctant to bestow mercies upon us. We know not why we do it, except that you have told us to ask for such things as we desire.

We ask you to grant to us that blessing that cannot be mistaken; that voice that can come only from him that speaks to the inmost consciousness. Grant to every one of us the incoming of your Spirit. Grant to every one a holy joy, a heavenly gladness. May every one feel that he is made the guest of God himself. And grant that all our offerings of song, and prayer, and meditation, and instruction, may be acceptable in your sight, and beneficial to us. May this year be marked by us as one of spiritual growth, and will you grant us such temporal prosperity as may be good for us. We ask it through Jesus, the Redeemer. Amen!

In Time of Affliction

O merciful God, and heavenly Father, who have taught us in your holy Word that you do not willingly afflict or grieve the children of men; look with pity, we ask you, upon the sorrows of your servants. In your wisdom, you have seen fit to visit us with trouble, and to bring distress upon us. Remember us, O Lord, in mercy; sanctify your fatherly correction to us; endue our souls with patience under our affliction, and with resignation to your blessed will; comfort us with a sense of your goodness, lift up your countenance upon us, and give us peace; through Jesus Christ our Lord. Amen!

In Winter

O God, who shuts up the earth in winter, that you may afterward visit and bless it: teach us by this your course in nature to trust you in your dealings with our souls. May we never be discouraged at the hiding of your face, nor cast away hope for want of inward comfort. Teach us that, as nature needs the check of the frost and the buffeting of the storm, so do we require your chastisements to keep down our pride, and seasons of trouble to establish and settle our faith. And as in due time your south wind blows, and you renew the face of the earth, so do you, O Lord, graciously carry on the work that you have begun in your servants. Return, O Lord, our strength, and lift up the light of your countenance upon us, and visit us with your salvation; through Jesus Christ our Lord. Amen!

For the Young on Uniting with the Church

Accept, we ask you, our Father, the consecration which you have inclined these our children to make of themselves to you this day. We thank you that they are beginning so early to serve you. We thank you that it is not the fragments of their life that they bring with them. We thank you that they have consecrated the dew of their youth to their God, and that they mean to live a life of purity, of love, of truth, of self-denial, and of activity for others. And we pray that the generous and godly purposes that have been inspired in their hearts, and have ripened into convictions and decisions in them, may be nourished by your grace, and perpetuated by your Spirit, which gave them birth. And may they never be ashamed of Christ or his cause. May they never be weary of well-doing. May they begin at once to do all the duty that is made known to then. May they have manifested in their hearts the truth of your word, that your yoke is easy and that your burden is light. May they have hope and courage inspired from the very beginning, by victories over easily besetting sins. And to your name shall be the praise, Father, Son and Spirit. Amen!

On the Birth of a Child

Life, O Lord, is from you, and the consecration of life is from you. May the new life committed to our care and love as a family be nurtured faithfully for you, and be ever in your gracious keeping. If the unconsciousness of infancy shall be followed by the intelligence of riper years, may that intelligence be taught of you, so that the heart may be a heart to serve you in this world, and to find its portion in you in the world to come. For your goodness and mercifulness in this event we thank you, and ask you to bow your ear to this our supplication, for the Savior's sake. Amen!

On a Missionary Occasion

O you great Shepherd of the sheep, who did come into this world to seek and to save that which was lost, and who has promised to gather your flock out of all the places where they have been scattered in the cloudy and dark day, we ask your blessing upon those who are laboring in your name among the unconverted of our own and other lands. Cheer you them in their hours of sadness and discouragement, and may their faith in your good promise never wholly fail. Shine in the dark places of the earth, O you, who are the light and life of men, until everywhere the fathers to the children shall make known your truth. Especially would we remember in our prayers those missionaries whose work is known to us, and to whose aid we stand pledged. May the example of their faithfulness and courage make us more generous and more self-denying; more ready to help, more glad to give; and unto you, with the Father and the Holy Spirit, shall be the glory, world without end. Amen!

On Behalf of Children

Heavenly Father, we bless you for the love of childhood as seen in Jesus Christ. Look, we ask you, upon the children of this family, and nurture them for yourself by the grace of your Holy Spirit. May they grow up to call you blessed. Guard them, we pray you, against the snares to which youth is ever exposed. So order their path for them that they may continually serve you. Be with them in all the unforeseen experiences of life, that aided by you in all their times of need, their home and heritage at last may be with the Redeemer. This, O Lord, we earnestly ask from you; in the name of Jesus Christ our Lord. Amen!

For a Sick Child

Most merciful Savior, who loves little children, and yourself did live as a little child upon the earth, we come to you in behalf of one whom we love. You are the Good Shepherd and care for the lambs of your flock, leading them tenderly and bearing them in your gentle arms, Bring you this child, for whom our prayer is offered, through the time of sickness and danger. Teach him to be meek and loving and obedient like yourself. Keep him from all fretfulness and impatience. Let him feel that you are ever near. Let him learn to love you better and better. And if you are pleased to restore him to health, make him to walk all his days, be they many or few, in the way that leads to eternal life. Hear us, O pitiful and loving Lord, who, with the Father and the Holy Spirit, live and reign one God, world without end. Amen!

On a Wedding Morning

We thank you, O Lord, for the circumstances and prospects of this happy morning, for the mutual affection you have kindled in the bosoms of those who are soon to be made one; for the suitability of their union; for the brightness of their hopes; and for the joy which fills them both. Do you sanction and bless their marriage. May he who was present at Cana of Galilee, and who turned the water into wine, be present at their nuptials, and crown with his favor our approaching festivities, and enhance these temporal mercies by the crowning gift of the Holy Spirit.

Lord, purify and hallow, guide and keep your servants this day, and throughout all the future years of their wedded life ; that amid its lights and shadows, its joys and sorrows, its duties and cares, they may evermore have affiance in you.

After safely passing through the pilgrimage of this world, may they attain to everlasting felicity in your immediate presence amid the holy angels, through Jesus Christ our Lord. Amen!

On Entering a New Home

O gracious Father, from whom comes every good and perfect gift, we thank you for this earthly home, into which we have come and where we are to abide for awhile. We pray that it may be to us a happy place, sanctified by your presence and your constant benediction; a refuge from the storm of worldly cares and temptations; a sanctuary of pure and holy affections; a center from which shall go out influences to bless other hearts and homes. May it be a place where those virtues which qualify the soul for the duties and trials of this life and for the joys of heaven, shall be fostered. Forbid, we ask you, O our heavenly Father, that the spirit of envy, of strife, of selfishness or of irreverence, should ever abide under this roof. May we dwell here in contentment in mutual esteem and helpfulness, in loving dependence upon your gracious bounty, and in constant, expectation of, and preparation for, that eternal, heavenly home, of which this is the type. May this become a dear spot to all of us, because of tender associations and hallowed influences, towards which fond memory shall turn in the oncoming years, when its present inmates shall no longer form one family group. We pray you to sanctify to us this home making, and consecrate this home to our use, and grant us all at last, a welcome to our Father's house in heaven; through the grace of our Lord Jesus Christ, to whom with you and the Holy Spirit, be glory forever. Amen!

THE LORD'S PRAYER

Our Father who is in Heaven, Hallowed be your Name. Your kingdom come. Your will be done on earth as it is in Heaven. Give us this day our daily bread. And forgive us our trespasses, as we forgive those who trespass against us. And lead us not into temptation: But deliver us from evil: For yours is the kingdom, and the power, and the glory, forever and ever. Amen!

Almighty God, who gives us grace with one accord to make our common supplications unto you; and did promise that when two or three are gathered together in your name you will grant their requests. Fulfill now, O Lord, the desire and petitions of your servants, as may be most expedient for them; grant us in this world knowledge of your truth; and in the world to come life everlasting. Amen!

Also Available

"To open *Communings in the Sanctuary* is to enter a vast, largely unexplored, field of 19th century piety. It comes as something of a shock to those who thought they knew their spiritual roots to find a book so completely animated by the love of God and the mystery of God... Taken slowly and meditatively, these masterpieces are sure to awaken the soul tot he joys of devotion."

Darryl Tippens, Provost, Pepperdine University

148 pages, $11.95 paper
To order call toll free **1-877-634-6004**